T0266993

THE NAPA VALLEY
LENDVEST
FRAUD SCANDAL

THE NAPA VALLEY LENDVEST
FRAUD SCANDAL

RAYMOND A. GUADAGNI

THE
History
PRESS

Published by The History Press
Charleston, SC
www.historypress.com

Copyright © 2024 by Raymond A. Guadagni
All rights reserved

Front cover, clockwise from top left: Calvin Robinson. *Courtesy of Norman Wood*; headlines from the *Napa Valley Register*. *Courtesy of Napa County Library Newspaper Archives*; David G. Hanson's mug shot following his arrest on Friday, December 22, 1989. *Courtesy of Napa County Sheriff's Department*; federal agents survey the boxes of marijuana and bags of hashish on the U.S. Coast Guard dock on Yerba Buena Island, San Francisco Bay. *Courtesy of Norman Wood*. *Back cover, top*: Yolo County Courthouse. *Courtesy of Yolo County*; *inset*: Napa Police sergeant Kris Dern. *Courtesy of the Napa Police Historical Society*.

First published 2024

Manufactured in the United States

ISBN 9781467156349

Library of Congress Control Number: 2024935399

Notice: The information in this book is true and complete to the best of our knowledge. It is offered without guarantee on the part of the author or The History Press. The author and The History Press disclaim all liability in connection with the use of this book.

All rights reserved. No part of this book may be reproduced or transmitted in any form whatsoever without prior written permission from the publisher except in the case of brief quotations embodied in critical articles and reviews.

This book is dedicated to all victims of financial fraud. It is my hope that those affected can heal and recover from the emotional and financial devastation of the fraud perpetrated on them. It is quite common for victims of scams to feel foolish and ashamed, but please know that victims of fraud are not at fault. Scam artists excel at using tactics that can trick anyone, and any shame belongs to them alone.

CONTENTS

CONTENTS

PREFACE

This book tells the story of two major crimes. These crimes covered an area of Northern California from the Sacramento delta to the San Francisco Bay to the community of Napa.

Part I describes a sensational drug bust in San Francisco Bay. While it was in and of itself monumental, its relevance here is how it led to the discovery of the financial fraud that caused the ruin of many Napa citizens. This part describes the drug smuggling operation and investigation and the resulting three trials in federal court. It further explains the connection between the drug bust and the money laundering (currency structuring) committed by principals in the LendVest Mortgage Company.

Part II is the essence of my work: the LendVest fraud case. It details the trial in the State of California fraud case against David Hanson, the founder and president of LendVest Mortgage Inc. and the most culpable perpetrator of the fraud.

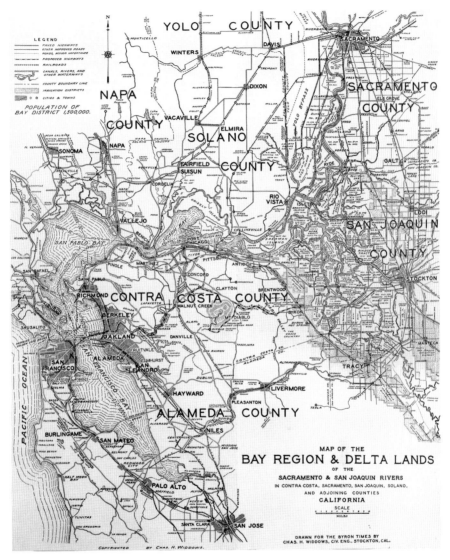

Map of the Bay Region and Delta Lands. This map illustrates the geographic proximity of the primary locations described within this book: the Sacramento River delta, the San Francisco Bay and the city of Napa. *Courtesy of Holt-Atherton Special Collections, University of the Pacific Library.*

ACKNOWLEDGEMENTS

I have received valuable help from many people in writing this book. First and foremost, I thank my wife, Ann, for her assistance, suggestions, support and the sacrifice of her time and effort in this endeavor. She gave her attention and her energy because she knew it was important to me. Without her, the book would not have been written. Simply thanking Ann is not enough, however. Ann has been the most important person in my life for the last forty-nine years—forty-nine years of sacrifice, forgiveness and real love. Ann is my rock.

I thank my friend Carolyn Woolston, editor *extraordinaire*. Beyond her exceptional skills as an editor and wordsmith, she was always there to support and encourage me.

My friend George Asbury was extraordinarily helpful in identifying and locating some of the victims of the LendVest fraud. I am grateful to all the people who allowed me to interview them. They gave up their valuable time and effort to provide me with their views and recollections of the events set forth in this book. Some of those recollections are painful for them to this day.

I appreciate my longtime friends Michael and Chyrle Crane and their nephew Alex Sneed for their time and efforts in locating and providing to me a videotape of a television news broadcast about the May 1988 drug bust.

Allison Haley, Napa County's district attorney, was a tremendous help in obtaining the case file. Her generosity of time and effort is deeply appreciated.

My heartfelt gratitude goes to retired judge Steven Kroyer, who was the prosecuting attorney in the LendVest case, and attorney Mervin Lernhart Jr., who defended David Hanson. As the opposing attorneys in the case, they freely provided me with their recollections of the courtroom legal battle between them.

Thanks also to Ed Wynn, retired police officer and investigator with the district attorney's office. He too is a friend and was always supportive with his recollections.

I also must give my sincere appreciation to retired sergeant Todd Shulman of the Napa Police Department. His assistance was invaluable in obtaining many photos I needed for the book.

Finally, I am immensely grateful to former special agent Norman Wood for his willingness to share with me the real story behind the drug smuggling operation.

PART I

THE DRUG TUG

1

THE DRUG BUST

On May 24, 1988, following a lengthy investigation, the Coast Guard stopped the tugboat *Intrepid Venture* and the barge it towed in the San Francisco Bay.

U.S. Customs agents subsequently seized more than forty-five tons of marijuana and hashish, valued at $189 million. The drugs reportedly had been loaded on the barge from a "mother ship" several hundred miles off the Hawaiian coast. The seizure of the drugs was said to be the largest in the world.

The drug containers were concealed beneath the deck under steel three-eighths of an inch thick that had been welded to the deck, according to U.S. Customs special agent Wayne Yamashita. It took eight hours for agents to cut welded metal covers off the compartments to remove the contraband. They found 1,400 plastic-wrapped cardboard boxes, weighing at least fifteen tons, filled with Southeast Asian marijuana and 1,200 burlap bags of pressed hashish weighing thirty-seven and a half tons, believed to be from Afghanistan.

Yamashita also said that Customs agents arrested five men after the U.S. Coast Guard boarded the *Intrepid Venture*:

1. CALVIN ROBINSON, forty-seven, whose business, Dredge Masters Associates, was located at 1063 Olive Hill Lane, just outside the Napa city limits. The tugboat and barge were owned by Robinson's business. Yamashita said Calvin Robinson reportedly was recently released from prison after serving a nineteen-year sentence.

2. FRANK ROBINSON, the nephew of Calvin Robinson, who gave a Corning, California address.
3. JOHN ROBINSON of Santa Rosa, California, also a nephew of Calvin.
4. WILLIAM ROBINSON, Calvin's son.
5. WESLEY BASTIN, Calvin Robinson's stepson, also of Corning.

The seventy-foot tug, based in Rio Vista, left San Francisco Bay with the barge in tow in early May, according to Assistant U.S. Attorney Steve Graham, head of the Organized Crime Drug Enforcement Task Force.

Drug agents tracked the vessels part of the way to the mother ship and back. The whereabouts of the mother ship remained unknown.

Federal agents were tipped off to the drug smuggling operations by Sergeant Kris Dern, commander of the Napa Special Investigation Bureau (NSIB). The NSIB is responsible for investigating illegal drug cases.

The tugboat *Intrepid Venture* pulling its barge in San Francisco Bay as it departed on its journey to pick up the drugs off the Hawaiian coastline. *Courtesy of Norman Wood.*

City of Napa Police sergeant Kris Dern. *Courtesy of the Napa Police Historical Society.*

Dern said an unidentified informant had contacted NSIB in 1987 with information about a Napa County smuggling operation involving vessels and a major drug haul happening offshore. Dern said the contact by the informant was about six to seven months prior to this event.

"I was given some names, some addresses, and told that there would be vessels involved," Dern said. "I checked out some of what was told to me, and it turned out to be accurate."

Once the information checked out locally, Dern, who had limited resources at his disposal—including only a small Napa patrol boat that could not go on the high seas—turned the investigation over to the Customs agents. "It was too big for me to handle in Napa County," Dern said. "The last I heard they were tracking a load on the open seas."

Officials were trying to figure out where and how the money was raised to buy the drugs. Investigators estimated ring members had to spend $15 million to purchase the drugs and transport them and could have grossed as much as $189 million. The U.S. Customs Service received information that in the summer of 1987, Calvin Robinson had paid "various crew members" $50,000 each for taking part in a multi-kilo hashish smuggling operation involving another tugboat. Agents speculated that the drug profits from this previous drug smuggling operation may have funded this most recent drug run.

Rollin B. Klink, special agent in charge for the U.S. Customs Service in San Francisco, said, "This was a very sophisticated operation." He characterized the organization behind the operation as "huge."

"This is by far the largest seizure the U.S. Customs Service has ever made," Yamashita said. "We're certain this whole investigation will have a nationwide impact."

The U.S. Customs Service was one of several federal agencies, including the Coast Guard, the Drug Enforcement Administration and the Internal Revenue Service, that participated in an investigation that spanned months.

Because Calvin Robinson, one of the suspects arrested for the drug bust, was from Napa, and based on information developed by Sergeant Dern from the Napa Special Investigations Bureau, a federal task force commenced investigating local Napa businesses with suspected financial ties to the drug trafficking ring.

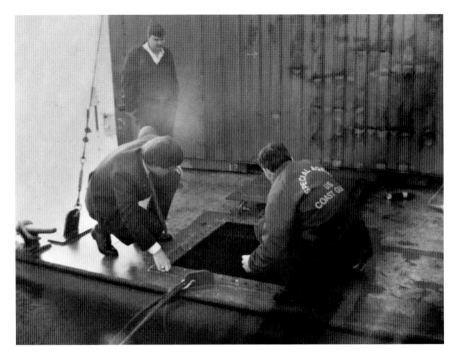

U.S. Coast Guard special agent in charge Rollin Klink (*right*) and U.S. Coast Guard agent Dale Carr on the barge following its seizure on May 24, 1988. *Courtesy of Norman Wood.*

They started with Calvin Robinson and Robinson family members connected with their business, Dredge Masters Associates.

The financial aspect of the investigation began in October 1987, some eight months prior to the drug bust in May 1988, because Napa Valley Bank officials had informed IRS agents of transactions by Calvin and his sister Diana Robinson Rauch involving large amounts of cash.

Calvin and Diana had opened a checking account with $5,000 in $100 bills, according to a high-ranking bank official. Before the account was closed two months later, $193,000 in $100 bills was moved through the checking account, the official said.

"We got wise to them and closed it (the account)," the official said.

With certain exceptions, such as supermarkets and certain other businesses that deal in large amounts of cash daily, banks are required to report all cash transactions of $10,000 or more. Federal law also requires banks to report all suspicious transactions involving large amounts of cash even if they don't, as in the Robinsons' case, reach that $10,000 threshold, the bank official said.

Calvin Robinson, a 1960 Napa High School graduate, reportedly had lived in Napa until moving to Corning, a small town in Tehama County, California, several months prior. Calvin Robinson had an extensive criminal record and had served nineteen years in prison. Age forty-seven at his arrest, Robinson was once charged with participating in a string of bank holdups by a gang that included convicted spy Christopher Boyce.

According to court documents, Robinson had been a prison cellmate of Boyce, who was convicted in 1977 of espionage for the Soviet Union. Robinson reportedly went on the lam with Boyce after his sensational January 19, 1980 escape from federal prison in Lompoc, California, where he was serving a forty-year sentence. The story of Boyce selling secret government information to the Soviet Union was told in the 1985 movie *The Falcon and the Snowman*. Robinson was charged with harboring a fugitive and in connection with thirteen Northwest bank robberies following Boyce's capture in late 1981. But the charges against Robinson were ultimately dismissed by U.S. District Judge Harold Ryan in Idaho for lack of evidence.

The drug smuggling investigation moved from Customs offices on Yerba Buena Island to Napa, when agents from the IRS and other federal investigators spent most of an entire day at 1063 Olive Hill Lane, near the Napa Valley Country Club. This house was the business address of Calvin Robinson's company, Dredge Masters Associates. It was also the residence of Sue Robinson Lemmons, Calvin's sister, and her husband, Don Lemmons. Investigators said Sue Lemmons did bookkeeping for Dredge Masters Associates.

The investigation quickly led agents to LendVest Mortgage Inc. of Napa, where Robinson's brother-in-law Donald Lemmons served as a vice president and corporate director, and from there to the Joseph Mathews Winery, which had extensive financial dealings with LendVest.

After further investigation, Don Lemmons and his wife, Sue Lemmons, were arrested at their home by federal agents. IRS agents said they seized $260,000 in cash and bank account assets from the Lemmonses. Financial records were also seized from the Lemmons house and businesses. At the time of the Lemmonses' arrest, Sue's brother Calvin Robinson remained in federal custody on the recent drug smuggling and money laundering charges. Sue's sister Diana Robinson Rauch, who was involved in their brother's business, had also been arrested.

Following the arrest of Don and Sue Lemmons, Steve Giorgi, chief of the criminal investigation division for the IRS, said that criminal "complaints were being drafted…charging the Lemmonses with structuring of currency transactions to avoid reporting requirements."

According to Giorgi, on five consecutive days, the Lemmonses had deposited more than $10,000 into their personal bank accounts.

Two Bank of America checking accounts belonging to Dredge Masters Associates with balances totaling $112,000 were also seized by IRS agents. Steve Giorgi said, "We have probable cause to believe the money in the accounts represents the proceeds of illegally structured currency transactions."

THE INVESTIGATION SPREADS

The investigation showed that the money laundering scandal had spread. According to federal investigators, the top two officers of LendVest Mortgage Inc. of Napa and the managing general partner of the Joseph Mathews Winery complex had helped the accused members of the Robinson family drug smuggling ring "launder" more than $200,000 in November 1987.

Besides the two top officers of LendVest there were twelve people, identified as LendVest employees, officers and close associates, who deposited large amounts of cash in their personal accounts in November 1987 and then wrote checks the same day to a LendVest corporate account at a Bank of America branch in Concord, federal documents alleged. That account was seized by the IRS agents pursuant to a court order. The account contained $169,000.

IRS agent Richard Carl, attached to Financial and Organized Crime Drug Enforcement task forces in San Francisco, identified three people involved in the money laundering:

1. DAVID G. HANSON, the president of LendVest Mortgage Inc. and its predecessor, Napa Valley Mortgage Inc. In his affidavit, Richard Carl stated that Hanson made three deposits totaling $25,000 in his personal account to LendVest in violation of the currency structuring laws under the provisions of a federal money laundering act.
2. DAVID F. DICKSON, LendVest's senior vice president and a neighbor of Donald and Sue Lemmons, who had already been arrested and charged with money laundering, conspiracy and being an accessory to drug smuggling. According to the affidavit, Dickson made two deposits totaling $19,200 and wrote three checks to LendVest totaling $30,000.

3. ROBERT PITNER, the managing partner of Joseph Mathews Winery Ltd., which operated the winery, the Sherry Oven restaurant and the Hennessey House bed-and-breakfast inn in Napa. Pitner, according to the affidavit of IRS agents, made two deposits to his personal accounts totaling $18,000 and wrote three checks to LendVest totaling $30,000. Investigation and county records showed that LendVest and its predecessor, Napa Valley Mortgage, had extensive financial dealings with the winery.

According to the affidavit filed by IRS agent Richard Carl, almost fifty currency transactions at financial institutions were made by these individuals acting in concert to avoid the filing of the required federal forms, and in many instances the currency was uncirculated sequentially numbered $100 bills.

The affidavit also alleged that on November 25, 1987, employees, officers and close associates of LendVest—including Sue Lemmons, Hanson, Pitner and Dickson—deposited a total of $200,000 in currency in personal bank accounts in Napa and Vallejo.

On the same day the deposits were made, $200,000 in checks payable to LendVest were written against the accounts into which the cash had been deposited. Many had the notation "Loan Payment" written in the memo portion of the check. The deposits were made in amounts equal to or less than $10,000.

IRS investigators had uncovered a pattern of transactions in which a few people (Sue Lemmons, David Hanson, David Dickson and Robert Pitner) connected to either Dredge Masters, LendVest or Mathews Winery made significant cash deposits into personal accounts and immediately wrote checks for similar amounts to LendVest. Each deposit involved sums of less than $10,000—the upper limit above what had to be reported to the IRS—but altogether totaled around $200,000. Investigators believed this evidence pointed strongly to money laundering (technically called currency structuring).

The U.S. Customs Service had a theory regarding the source of the money involved in the laundering. They believed that a different tugboat, the *Ruby R*, had been used in 1987 by Calvin Robinson to smuggle thirty tons of Afghanistan hashish into the San Francisco area. The owner of the *Ruby R* was Merle Robinson, Calvin Robinson's estranged wife, according to Quint Villanueva, Pacific regional commissioner of the Customs Service.

The tugboat *Ruby R* allegedly used by Calvin Robinson in a prior drug smuggling operation in 1987. *Courtesy of Norman Wood.*

Customs agents further believed that the money made from this previous trip in 1987 was laundered and used for purchasing the drugs seized in the May 1988 drug bust of the *Intrepid Venture* tugboat.

Lawyers for the defendants in the drug bust and the related money laundering charges publicly criticized federal authorities. One lawyer, Frank Bell, said, "The government has engaged in incredible overreaching. They have seized virtually every known asset that's owned by my client, Calvin Robinson or his family….They have tied his hands behind his back and are attempting to kick him in his private parts."

The attorney said the effect of this was to hamper any attempt of Calvin Robinson to fight the charges or fight the attempt to hold him without bail.

Federal prosecutor Eric Swenson told reporters that Bell's accusations were "baloney." Swenson said, "The assets that we've seized are all drug-related or are involved in money laundering." The prosecutor added, "If Mr. Robinson is losing his assets, it's because he gained them through illegal activity."

Another defense lawyer, Bernard Segal, who represented Sue Lemmons, criticized the seizures. He said Dredge Masters, of which his client was corporate secretary, was a "legitimate dredging business" that grossed $3.5 million last year and held contracts with the U.S. Army Corps of Engineers.

Segal said, "With their assets in government hands, the defendants have no way of defending themselves in this criminal case."

The defendants started to turn on each other as well.

Robert Pitner's attorney claimed that his client was duped. Pitner's lawyer, John Milano of San Francisco, said, "There is nothing illegal about a person not wanting to cause a currency transaction report to be filed. If there had been something illegal here, it would require knowing that these funds were illegally acquired or that there was some illegal purpose in depriving the government of the information."

Milano said his client admitted that he used his personal bank account to transfer $30,000 of the $200,000 in cash that federal investigators tied to money laundering for accused drug smuggling members of the Napa-based Robinson family. However, Milano denied that Pitner, who was the managing general partner of the Joseph Mathews Winery complex in Napa, knew the source of the cash and said Pitner was duped by the president of LendVest, David Hanson.

Milano said that Hanson told Pitner that the money represented the proceeds of an insurance settlement members of a family were investing in LendVest. Hanson told Pitner that he should make the investment deposit because the family did not want to do it themselves.

Because Pitner did not know that something illegal was going on, Milano argued that what Pitner did was not illegal. He did not know the funds were illegally acquired. Milano said, "He was misled into doing a favor for someone, unknowingly used to help structure this transaction."

2

THE COLLAPSE OF LENDVEST
AND JOSEPH MATHEWS WINERY

In addition to federal agents investigating connections between the drug smuggling and businesses such as LendVest and the Joseph Mathews Winery, real estate auditors began inspecting LendVest's books. The IRS opened an office in Napa and requested public assistance in the investigation of the drug smuggling ring that involved allegations of money laundering by LendVest officials.

Meanwhile, LendVest investors claimed that they had been stymied in attempts to withdraw their money from LendVest because the officers had been tied to the accused members of the Robinson family.

The investors said LendVest officials blamed the delay on the IRS investigation. But the IRS rebutted this claim, saying that it had not seized or encumbered any LendVest assets other than the confiscation of $189,000 from the Bank of America account believed by agents to be laundered drug profits received from a member of the Robinson family.

Concurrently with the various state and federal organizations investigating LendVest, by June 1, 1988, Napa County district attorney Jerry Mautner said he would be asking the federal government to begin a racketeering investigation of LendVest Mortgage Inc.

Mautner said if the U.S. Attorney's Office opted not to enter the case, he might ask the major fraud unit of the California Attorney General's Office to investigate. Mautner did say that his office lacked the resources to conduct its own criminal investigation. "The feds have the case, and the IRS can't give us any information."

The LendVest corporate offices were formerly located in this building located at 1957 Sierra Avenue in Napa. *Photo by the author.*

By now, LendVest was being besieged by investors inquiring about their investments and demanding to withdraw their money.

The company's board replaced its chief officers in June 1988, electing a slate led by David Dickson, the senior vice president, to replace David Hanson, who was ousted as president. A company spokesman said the shift was the result of the federal drug smuggling investigation that linked Hanson, Dickson and other LendVest officials to allegations of money laundering. The spokesman was Jeffrey Moore, who was promoted from vice president to chief financial officer. Moore said that the board felt there was a strong need

The LendVest Mortgage Company offices were formerly located in this building at 2800 Jefferson Street in Napa. *Photo by the author.*

to have company leaders who were not tied to the investigation make the attempt to resolve the concerns of LendVest's customers. However, Moore was unable to explain how changing the top officers could accomplish a resolution. He did say he was giving 100 percent of his time to the problems of the organization.

But when investors wanted a more complete explanation of the company's situation, Moore responded, "The hysteria is not helpful, not that I don't understand."

Moore told investors to stay calm. "People don't want to work themselves up to the point of jeopardizing their well-being and health. It's entirely possible they could do that."

Moore said it was important that state and federal investigators be given time to come up with the facts. "I tell our investors we have nothing that leads us to believe their money isn't safe," he said. "I know my portion of the business and believe it to be solid." Moore went on to say that LendVest wouldn't have grown as rapidly as it had if its mortgage and banking practices were not reputable.

Moore pointed out that LendVest had been approved by the Veterans Administration the previous year for automatic approval of mortgage loans. "That comes from eight years of a spotless track record," Moore said.

However, Moore said, the flood of requests by LendVest investors who wanted their money back exceeded the company's ability to respond even in normal times, and especially when the IRS confiscated the money from the Bank of America account.

Despite Moore's best efforts, on Wednesday June 1, 1988, LendVest laid off all seventy-three employees and put 90 percent of its business up for sale after losing a $5 million line of credit.

Moore said, "LendVest couldn't pay its seventy-three employees after losing its major source of mortgage loan funds." This line of credit provided 90 percent of the company's operating capital. With most of its business up for sale, it was a foregone conclusion that the entire staff would have to be laid off.

Moore further said that LendVest had received offers from "two or three major banking firms" interested in taking over the portion of LendVest's business formerly financed by Bank of America. That would leave LendVest primarily with trust accounts that made up 10 percent of its business, according to Moore.

But no sales came to fruition. While LendVest continued to attempt to sell its mortgage banking business, investors grew tired of waiting and hired lawyers who began to examine the possibility of filing suit to force what remained of LendVest into bankruptcy to protect their clients' interests.

Finally, a Napa woman who invested $38,000 with LendVest Mortgage Inc. filed suit in Napa Superior Court against LendVest alleging she was defrauded out of her life's savings.

The suit was filed by Jerri A. Johnson of Napa and named LendVest and its officers—including ousted president David G. Hanson—as defendants. Johnson alleged that LendVest officials took money from her and other investors "for the sole purpose of using such funds for unlawful purposes." According to the lawsuit, efforts to get repayment of her investment had failed because all LendVest assets had been seized or frozen by state and federal regulatory agencies. The lawsuit was filed by Sonoma attorney Steven W. Linthicum.

In addition, the lawsuit declared that Hanson provided Johnson with a property synopsis declaring that her investment was secured by a second deed of trust on LendVest's corporate office building, 1957 Sierra Avenue, in Napa. But the suit alleged that LendVest officials breached her investment agreement and never secured her investment.

The allegations in the lawsuit were for breach of contract, negligence, breach of fiduciary duty and conspiracy. The suit sought her original investment, court costs, attorney fees and $100,000 in punitive damages.

Spokesman Jeffrey Moore was concerned that this suit was going to open the floodgates to more civil suits or possibly petitions to drive LendVest into bankruptcy.

Moore tried to stem off this flood of anticipated lawsuits and bankruptcy. He indicated that the company would prefer an unofficial reorganization with participation of the investors. He said that filing for protection from creditors under federal bankruptcy laws remained a possibility, but forcing the company into bankruptcy would only reduce the possibility of investors getting their money. Moore said this was because assets would be diminished by legal and court fees.

Unsecured investors called a meeting with LendVest officials to discuss next steps. At that meeting, the officials proposed their plan for unofficial reorganization of the company instead of going through the bankruptcy court.

Investors, however, were worried about the safety of their investments, since the company was linked with the accused Robinson family drug ring and the allegations by federal officials that LendVest officials laundered money through company accounts. In fact, during this time LendVest had all but collapsed in the wake of the allegations that the Lemmonses and several other officers engaged in a plot to launder profits linked to the drug smuggling.

Ultimately, the investors rejected the proposal of the LendVest officials, and on June 14, 1988, a group of five investors filed suit to force the company into involuntary bankruptcy. The five investors were all represented by Steve Linthicum, the attorney who was representing Jerri Johnson in her Napa suit to recover her initial investment ($38,000) plus punitive damages based on fraud. The five petitioners in the bankruptcy filing were Elaine and John Richter of Vallejo, Ronald M. Walker, Jerri A. Johnson and Louise Kraus, all of Napa.

Linthicum's case for the five investors was different because it involved filing a petition against LendVest under Chapter 7 of the federal bankruptcy law. Chapter 7 permits the court to determine whether a company is bankrupt and, if so, to dissolve the company and divide its assets among creditors.

The petition on behalf of these five investors was for a total of $580,000 in unsecured investments.

Elaine Richter, a spokeswoman for the investors, said that when the investors heard the petitioners' reasons for their decision, they supported the bankruptcy petition "overwhelmingly." She said the unofficial reorganization as proposed by LendVest was "just too much responsibility."

Ms. Richter explained that "there were grave matters we would be called on to decide, and at this point, they are beyond the abilities of the self-appointed investors committee."

She clarified, "We would need expertise regarding record searches, distribution of the secured deeds of trust…closing some offices, leaving others open…deciding who to borrow from…and the personal liability of the committee members."

Lawyers for the investors advised that bankruptcy court was not necessarily a bad place to end up. Richter said, "They told us it probably would have happened anyway." Further, the investors' advisors felt that bankruptcy court would protect rights of unsecured investors better than a reorganization.

Another plus with bankruptcy proceedings for the investors would be to avoid a continued dilution of the company's funds. The investors felt assets of LendVest would, if approved by the federal bankruptcy court, be under the direction of a court-appointed trustee.

It appeared that LendVest was in a precarious financial position. After the ouster of Hanson, the remaining officials divulged that the company had an estimated $10 million in assets and $14 million in liabilities.

A bankruptcy court hearing on whether to appoint a bankruptcy trustee was set for June 24, 1988.

The *Napa Valley Register* published an article about the case and included the advice of Ms. Richter that investors should submit proof of claim forms to the bankruptcy court as soon as possible.

The Pressure Increases

With LendVest's demise and the plunge into bankruptcy, the pressure intensified on Joseph Mathews Winery complex. The complex included the winery itself, the Sherry Oven restaurant and the Hennessy House bed-and-breakfast inn.

On June 6, 1988, Robert Pitner, the general managing partner of the complex, closed the Sherry Oven restaurant portion of the complex and laid off more than seventy employees. He indicated that he would try to find a buyer for the restaurant and bar. However, the facts showed that the entire complex, which included the inn and restaurant, had been losing money ever since its opening in 1986. The complex had relied heavily on LendVest and its investors for capital; Hanson even had a personal financial stake in the winery.

One month after Pitner closed the Sherry Oven restaurant portion of the complex, the entire Joseph Mathews Winery complex filed for Chapter 11 bankruptcy protection. A Chapter 11 bankruptcy provides for reorganization of a corporation or partnership. The chapter 11 debtor proposes a plan of reorganization to keep their business alive and pay creditors over time, as opposed to a Chapter 7 bankruptcy, which is a complete liquidation of the business and a division of assets among the creditors.

The anger of investors grew, and terms such as *fraud* and *intentional misrepresentation* were frequently being used by the frustrated investors, who were coming to the realization that they might lose their entire investments.

Not only were some civil fraud lawsuits being filed, but the investor groups were also examining the possibility of a civil fraud suit under federal Racketeer Influenced and Corrupt Organizations Act (usually known as RICO).

When the case finally landed in front of a bankruptcy judge, the involuntary petition filed against LendVest to liquidate its assets was stayed. The judge, Alan Jaroslovski, ordered that the troubled company be allowed a thirty-day period to attempt to reorganize under a court-appointed trustee.

The judge further ruled that if the attempt to reorganize failed, then the involuntary petition filed by the investors the previous week would be reinstated and the judge would then rule on the creditors' petition to liquidate LendVest's assets to recover their money.

The first hearing in the federal bankruptcy case was in a courtroom packed by eighty-eight spectators, many of them investors who took a chartered bus from Napa. At least a dozen lawyers and newspaper and television reporters were also in attendance.

The building that housed the former Sherry Oven Restaurant at the Joseph Mathews Winery complex. The complex is now under different ownership. *Photo by the author.*

After granting the transfer of the case under the federal bankruptcy code from Chapter 7 (dissolution petition, favored by the investors) to Chapter 11 (reorganization, favored by LendVest lawyers), Judge Jaroslovsky named Charles Duck of Santa Rosa to run LendVest for at least the next thirty days as the court-appointed trustee.

Duck was a professional bankruptcy creditor's trustee from Santa Rosa with seventeen years of experience in bankruptcy court. He had offices in San Francisco, Oakland and Santa Rosa. His job now would be to decide if LendVest could keep operating or should be liquidated to pay off creditors.

The conversion motion (to move the bankruptcy case from Chapter 7 to Chapter 11) was filed by LendVest's lawyer, Dennis Montali, who told Jaroslovski that LendVest expected $20,000 to $50,000 in revenue in the next thirty days.

The transfer to Chapter 11 was opposed by Steven Linthicum, the Sonoma lawyer who filed the federal bankruptcy suit for the five LendVest investors and was representing one of them in a damage suit in Napa County Superior Court.

Linthicum told Judge Jaroslovski that "this will result in a great deal of unnecessary expense; there's nothing to keep LendVest going. LendVest should be liquidated now. That's the way it will end up."

Opposite: The Hennessy House bed-and-breakfast that was formerly part of the Joseph Mathews Winery Complex. The bed-and-breakfast inn is currently operated by different owners. *Photo by the author.*

Right: The former Joseph Mathews Winery complex. *Photo by the author.*

Linthicum's warning to the judge was prescient.

Eventually, LendVest did go into Chapter 7 for full liquidation of all its assets. This did not happen before a series of continuances by LendVest lawyers prevented an immediate liquidation of assets. The series of continuances sought by LendVest and granted by the judge may have caused more damage to the creditors. Immediate liquidation of assets, however, might have benefited creditors. As it turned out, none of these continuances proved helpful to LendVest's desire for a reorganization. Further, the converse was also true: these delays were of no benefit to the investors.

3

THE CHARLES DUCK SCANDAL

There would be no luck for the investors in this case except bad luck. Things went from bad to worse. To understand the turn of events, it is important to understand the role of a bankruptcy creditor's trustee.

A bankruptcy trustee's primary role is to liquidate the debtor's (in this case, LendVest) assets in a manner that maximizes the return to the debtor's unsecured creditors. The trustee accomplishes this by gathering the debtor's assets (money, stocks, bonds, real estate, etc.) and passing it through to the creditors. The trustee has broad powers over this property. Not only can he sell the debtor's property, but he also has the authority to set aside prefential transfers made illegally to creditors within ninety days before the petition, among other actions. The trustee can pursue claims such as fraudulent conveyances. The trustee can even operate the business of the debtor if such operation would benefit creditors and enhance liquidation of the estate.

A bankruptcy trustee, with the powers he has over the debtor, can be of great benefit to creditors. But to be a benefit to the creditors, it is presupposed that the trustee is honest.

In a bizarre turn of events, it turned out that Charles Duck, the court-appointed trustee in the LendVest case, had refused to turn documents relating to Duck's trustee account at Exchange Bank over to U.S. Bankruptcy Court trustee Anthony Sousa even though he was court ordered to do so. And as luck would have it, one of Duck's cases was LendVest.

The order to Duck by Judge Lloyd King, chief bankruptcy judge, was to deliver these records to federal officials investigating activities in four bankruptcy cases in Sonoma County. This order was made because there was an ongoing investigation into allegations that Duck mishandled some bankruptcy cases. In fact, Trustee Sousa informed Duck that he had "discussed the case with U.S. Attorney Joseph Russoniello and that he would in all likelihood make a formal referral to the U.S. Attorney's Office" that might result in prosecution.

Court records indicated Duck had also been under investigations for (1) obtaining $400,000 in personal home loans from Redwood Bank of Napa, the same bank he used for his trustee accounts; (2) Duck's relationship to a management company used in bankruptcy case; and (3) questions concerning a vineyard he owned near Healdsburg.

Trustee Anthony Sousa contended that in the four bankruptcies under investigation, Duck had advanced funds in each case through the Exchange Bank account. He also said, "Duck's unorthodox practice of lending money to Chapter 7 and 11 estates placed him in the position of being a creditor of the very same estates he has pledged to administer and protect. This practice is inconsistent with the provisions of the bankruptcy code and creates an irreconcilable conflict of interest."

For example, Duck had made thirteen advances in the LendVest mortgage case, but Sousa said Duck couldn't determine if the total was $90,500 or $105,000. Also, in the LendVest case, Duck reported $32,408 as being repaid (to himself), but on another occasion, Sousa said, "the amount was $47,408."

Sousa said he also believed Duck's advances, or loans, were made without notices to the parties involved and without court authority. Nor were any "payments back to Duck made with court approvals," he added.

Clearly, on top of all the other problems for the LendVest investors, they engaged the bankruptcy court for their protection and drew a trustee who, at the least, was not disclosing the nature of his transactions and did not appear to be reporting his dealings accurately or with any degree of consistency.

Duck appeared before a federal judge and asked to delay the court order against him to turn over bankruptcy case records sought by the U.S. Bankruptcy Trustee's Office.

However, federal judge Stanley Weigel refused to delay the court order against Duck to turn over the records. The result of this denial by the judge meant that the previous court order to turn over documents had to be complied with by the end of business that very day. Duck still failed to comply with the order.

Those documents included LendVest records.

The documents Duck did not turn over meant Duck would now face charges for being in violation of the court's order. What was Duck's next move?

A little over a week passed after the court ordered Duck to hand over the records, and Charles Duck suddenly resigned from all his bankruptcy cases, including LendVest.

LendVest's creditors and investors had been unhappy with Duck for months because they felt he had been lackadaisical in handling the LendVest case. The LendVest creditors believed that Duck had spent large amounts of the company's funds but failed to receive any money. They also felt that Duck had kept the LendVest business offices open longer than necessary, further depleting funds that might otherwise have gone to the creditors. However, they were unaware of the real reason behind Duck's resignation until September 1989, when he was arraigned for embezzling $1.9 million from the assets he had managed as a bankruptcy trustee.

After Duck's resignation as trustee, the bankruptcy court appointed a new trustee to take over the LendVest case as well as other cases formerly under Duck's jurisdiction.

Charles E. "Chuck" Sims, veteran court reporter and owner of a deposition reporting business in Napa, was appointed successor trustee in the LendVest Mortgage Company bankruptcy.

In Sims's first appearance in the bankruptcy court on a LendVest matter, he said, "As I strode to the bench to begin the proceedings, the courtroom was packed. Most of those, I assume, were investors and creditors of LendVest. They stood and gave me a round of applause just because, I guess, I wasn't Charles Duck. I felt so bad for these people. I was committed to do the very best I could to help them."

Sims told newspaper reporters that he planned to hire new counsel—specifically the Santa Rosa firm of Geary, Shea, O'Donnell & Grattan—as well as the Napa firm of Lehman and Lehman as new certified public accountants "to go after whoever I have to go after."

Sims did say that he planned to be thrifty, "so the creditors can get something for their money." He expected to collect on judgments already

New trustee appointed in LendVest bankruptcy

Charles E. Sims, veteran court reporter and owner of a deposition reporting business in Napa, has been appointed successor trustee in the LendVest Mortgage Company bankruptcy.

Sims' appointment was made by U. S. Trustee Anthony G. Sousa. He succeeds Santa Rosa's Charles Duck, who resigned the post recently.

Sims said he plans to hire new counsel — the Santa Rosa firm of Geary-Shea & O'Donnell & Grattan — and new certified public accountants — the Napa firm of Lehman and Lehman — "to go after whoever I have to go after."

Sims said he plans to be thrifty, "so the creditors can get something for their money." He expects to collect on judgments already entered and to file new suits if necessary to return as much money as possible to LendVest investors.

Sims said today he is in the process of posting a $1 million bond as required by the U.S. Bankruptcy Court in Santa Rosa.

The LendVest criminal trial in San Francisco was expected to go to the jury today or Monday, bringing the conspiracy and money laundering case to a close.

Attorneys were presenting closing arguments in federal court in San Franciso this afternoon to a jury of six women and six men.

Opposite: Bankruptcy trustee Charles E. "Chuck" Sims was appointed to replace Charles Duck after he resigned as trustee. *Courtesy of the Sims family.*

Above: Headline from the June 2, 1989 edition of the *Napa Valley Register* announcing Charles E. Sims's appointment as bankruptcy trustee. *Courtesy of the Napa County Library Newspaper Archives.*

entered and to file new suits if necessary to return as much money as possible to LendVest investors. Sims said he would also post a $1 million bond as required by the U.S. Bankruptcy Court in Santa Rosa.

So, what happened to Charles Duck and the legal proceedings against him? The U.S. Trustees' Office had been investigating Duck for about one year. They found he comingled funds of the bankruptcy cases he oversaw with his own personal and business accounts and made loans to the businesses without properly notifying creditors and without court authority.

Other reports said Duck, who himself had a string of personal business failures, used the bankruptcy system to support an extravagant lifestyle and purchase valuable properties. Investigators said that between 1983 and 1989, Duck apparently took money for his personal expenses from the accounts of the businesses to which he was assigned trustee.

Left: Steven Olsen, attorney for bankruptcy trustee Charles E. "Chuck" Sims. *Courtesy of Steven Olsen.*

Below: Headline from the January 22, 1990 edition of the *Napa Valley Register* reporting that former bankruptcy trustee Charles Duck was sentenced to twenty-seven months in prison for embezzling $1.9 million from the cases he was assigned to handle. *Courtesy of the Napa County Library Newspaper Archives.*

Charles Duck sentenced to 27 months in prison

SAN FRANCISCO – Charles Duck, the former U.S. Bankruptcy Court trustee who pleaded guilty to embezzling $1.9 million from the cases he was assigned to handle, was sentenced Friday to 27 months in prison.

Duck, 56, of Santa Rosa, who served for a time as bankruptcy trustee for LendVest Mortgage Co. of Napa, also was fined $5,000.

According to the U.S. Trustees' office, which began investigating Duck one year ago, he co-mingled funds of the cases with his own personal and business accounts and made loans to the businesses without properly notifying creditors.

Reports said Duck, who himself had a string of personal business failures, used the bankruptcy system to support an extravagant lifestyle and purchase valuable properties.

Investigators said Duck apparently took money between 1983 and 1989 for his personal expenses from the accounts of the businesses to which he was assigned trustee.

Duck resigned from the bankruptcy court last spring. The U.S. Trustees office has not said whether any of the money which Duck embezzled came from LendVest Mortgage Co. and Duck was not charged with any violations specifically relating to the company.

Creditors of the once-prosperous Napa based mortgage company had long complained about Duck's handling of the case, claiming he was frittering away the company's already depleted assets.

Ultimately, Duck pleaded guilty to two counts of embezzlement, although it was not revealed at the time whether LendVest was among the accounts Duck had cheated. As the new trustee, Chuck Sims tried to determine what, if any, funds were taken by Duck from LendVest. Sims's attorney, Steven Olsen, later said Duck's embezzlement did not actually reach LendVest's money. It probably would have extended to LendVest's assets had Duck remained in office, but he did not. Still, the news of an embezzling trustee brought no comfort to the LendVest creditors.

On Friday, January 19, 1990, Duck was sentenced to twenty-seven months in prison. He was also fined $5,000.

4

THE FEDERAL INDICTMENTS

I n addition to the Drug Tug and money laundering charges already filed against Calvin Robinson and his crew for drug smuggling, indictments were now formally filed in federal court for unlawful currency structuring and conspiracy against the following individuals:

DAVID HANSON on one count of conspiracy, five counts of unlawful structuring of currency transactions and one count of failing to file a currency transaction report.

DAVID DICKSON on one count of conspiracy and one count of unlawful structuring. Dickson had just been named president of LendVest after Hanson was ousted in a company reorganization only two weeks before. He resigned this position after being indicted.

ROBERT PITNER on one count of conspiracy and one count of unlawful structuring.

DONALD LEMMONS, former chief appraiser and vice president of LendVest, on one count of conspiracy and one count of unlawful structuring.

SUE LEMMONS, Donald's wife and the secretary of Dredge Masters Associates, on one count of conspiracy and five counts of unlawful structuring.

DIANA (ROBINSON) RAUCH, sister of Calvin Robinson and Sue Lemmons and part owner of Dredge Masters, on one count of conspiracy and three counts of unlawful structuring.

Calvin L. Robinson, brother of Sue Lemmons and Diana (Robinson) Rauch, on one count of conspiracy and four counts of unlawful structuring.

Dredge Masters Associates, on one count of conspiracy and three counts of unlawful structuring.

LendVest Mortgage Inc., on one count of conspiracy, one count of unlawful structuring and one count of failure to file currency transaction reports.

The indictments were based on extensive research by the federal prosecutors. The details of how the prosecution reached its decision on who and what to charge in the indictments came from its investigation of a nine-month chronology of events. The result led to a federal grand jury's twenty-page, twelve-count indictment against the five men, two women and two Napa-based corporations.

The investigation showed that during the nine months between August 7, 1987, and May 24, 1988, multiple cash deposits ranging from $5,000 to more than $200,000 were made into various Bay Area banks by the defendants and other employees of LendVest. The evidence indicated a monthslong pattern of unlawful currency structuring and supported the charges of conspiracy between the defendants.

For example, during the month of August 1987, Sue Lemmons made seven deposits totaling $80,000 into a Dredge Masters' account at the El Sobrante branch of Bank of America. She made eight deposits totaling $74,000 into that same Dredge Masters account throughout September 1987.

During the month of October 1987, forty-two deposits totaling $228,000 were made by Sue Lemmons, Calvin Robinson, Diana Robinson Rauch and Dredge Masters into accounts they held in three banks: Bank of America, Security Pacific Bank and Napa Valley Bank. In the month of November, another twenty-seven deposits totaling $134,000 were made into the same three banks by these same defendants. Additionally, on October 14, 1987, Calvin Robinson and his sister Diana Robinson Rauch opened a Napa Valley Bank checking account with $5,000 in uncirculated $100 bills.

On November 24, 1987, Calvin Robinson and Donald and Sue Lemmons transferred $200,000 in currency to David Hanson, then president of LendVest Mortgage. Hanson then signed a fraudulent note for $200,000 payable to "Robinson, a partnership."

The very next day, November 25, 1987, LendVest vice president David Dickson received $29,000 of the $200,000 in cash received by Hanson. He then deposited the money into personal checking accounts he held with Napa Valley Bank, Napa National Bank and Vintage Bank.

On that same day, Joseph Mathews Winery Complex managing general partner Robert Pitner received $27,500 of the $200,000 in cash received by Hanson, which he then deposited into accounts he held with Bank of America, Redwood Bank and Vintage Bank.

Also on November 25, 1987, David Hanson deposited $25,000 of the $200,000 he received into personal checking accounts he held with Napa Valley Bank, Bank of America and Napa National Bank.

Finally, on November 25,1987, Hanson gave LendVest employees what was described in the indictment as "large amounts of currency." He asked the employees to deposit the money in their personal checking accounts and then remit the same amount by check to LendVest.

Throughout December 1987, Calvin Robinson and Diana Robinson Rauch made sixteen deposits totaling $80,000 into accounts they held at Napa Valley Bank and Security Pacific Bank.

On May 24, 1988—the day the Drug Tug was seized in San Francisco Bay by federal agents—Sue Lemmons withdrew $160,000 from Dredge Masters' checking accounts at Bank of America, including $118,000 in blank travelers' checks, a $32,000 cashier's check payable to Hanson and $10,000 in blank money orders.

Regarding the effect of the indictments and arrests on the Napa business community, the federal prosecutor, Swenson, said, "It was inevitable the house of cards would have to fall."

By the time of the indictments, U.S. Customs agents had already seized the record $189 million in drugs from the *Intrepid Venture*, and federal agents had now seized more than $800,000 from the Lemmonses' personal assets, LendVest and Dredge Masters Associates.

Lawyers were appointed by the court to represent all the defendants. All the defendants entered not guilty pleas.

The federal investigation was examined by federal prosecutors and arranged according to two categories.

The first category contained the facts pertaining to the May 1988 drug bust. This category would be against the captain of the tugboat, Calvin Robinson, and his crew. The prosecutors believed they did not have sufficient evidence to tie the money to either the May 1988 drug shipment or to a similar shipment believed to have occurred in August 1987. Accordingly, the prosecutors believed they could indict Calvin Robinson and his crew of the *Intrepid Venture* only on charges directly related to drug smuggling.

The second category included facts on charges of conspiracy and currency structuring. Indictments on these charges were against David Hanson, Robert Pitner, Dave Dickson, Sue and Don Lemmons, Calvin Robinson and his sister Diana Robinson Rauch.

Therefore, there would be two federal trials: one for drug smuggling and one for conspiracy and currency structuring.

5

TRIAL NUMBER ONE

DRUG SMUGGLING CHARGES AGAINST CALVIN ROBINSON

The first trial in federal court was for drug smuggling, and only Calvin Robinson and his crew were on trial for those charges.

The trial was before district judge John P. Vukasin. Vukasin was known as a no-nonsense judge who kept his proceedings moving on a tight schedule. Vukasin was willing to work long days to stay on track. He was also viewed as more of a law-and-order conservative than a judicial liberal.

Pretrial motions were heard by Vukasin. He denied a barrage of motions by defense attorneys that included requests for continuations of the trial, separate trials for each defendant and suppression of evidence relating to prior criminal records of some of the defendants. However, in a major ruling for the defense, Vukasin told the prosecuting attorneys that they would not be allowed to tell the jury about an earlier smuggling run allegedly made by members of the Robinson family in 1987. This was a significant ruling for the defense because it would have shown that the defendants had knowledge of the operation when they later served as crew members of a tug and barge in May 1988 on which federal agents found fifty-seven tons of hashish and marijuana.

The prosecutor pleaded with Vukasin not to rule out this evidence. Nevertheless, the judge ruled that this evidence could not come in against the defendants. There was no real evidence connecting the first drug smuggling operation with the second one. The defendants were happy with the ruling, but U.S. prosecutors Matt Pavone and Laurie Kloster-Gray strenuously argued that they had evidence that two of the defendants, Wesley Bastin and John Robinson, had set up hashish sales, bought expensive cars and flashed rolls of new $100 bills months before the alleged drug sale in May 1988 for which the five men were on trial. In fact, Pavone said the judge's ruling would reduce the prosecution's evidence by one-third.

Based on the judge's rulings, the prosecution took a simplistic view of how to prosecute those accused of drug smuggling. To obtain a conviction against Calvin Robinson and his crew, the prosecution believed they would have to show that Calvin Robinson and his relatives conspired to smuggle drugs into the country and then attempted to do so. If they could do those two things, they would win.

The first trial was set to proceed. However, at the beginning of this first trial, Calvin Robinson fired his attorneys and told the judge he wished to represent himself. The judge granted this request. The lawyers for the crew members then raised an objection to the judge, expressing their concern that the jury might be prejudiced against their clients because they were all represented by attorneys and Calvin was not. Accordingly, they requested a separate trial from Calvin, which the judge granted.

This meant the trial, which had commenced, now had to be brought to an abrupt halt with the present jury being excused. The proceedings would have to be continued for several weeks with a new jury being summoned. With separate trials being ordered, there would now be two trials on drug smuggling charges alone—one against Calvin Robinson and one against his crew. The third trial on currency violations and conspiracy would be conducted months later.

The Second Trial of Calvin Robinson Begins

The second attempt at the drug smuggling trial commenced in February 1989 and was now solely against Calvin Robinson, acting as his own attorney.

Prosecutor Laurie Kloster-Gray, in her opening statement to the jury, said the alleged drug run was "a carefully conceived and cleverly executed plan with one glitch—Mr. Robinson was caught red-handed. This load was worth hundreds of millions of dollars."

She described how, based on information they had received, U.S. Customs agents set up reconnaissance on Calvin Robinson and his relatives to survey what he was up to. They watched Robinson and his relatives spend months preparing the *Intrepid Venture* and the barge for the voyage.

According to Kloster-Gray, Robinson moored the barge at a remote island in Seven Mile Slough near Isleton in Solano County. She said the agents observed Robinson and his crew outfitting the tug, which hadn't been a seagoing vessel, with extra fuel tanks and high-tech navigational equipment. Such enhancements could indicate an intention to take the tugboat on the high seas.

During her opening statement, the prosecutor also explained to the jury that the *Intrepid Venture* left San Francisco Bay on May 6 and that Calvin Robinson told marine traffic controllers they were headed for Eureka in California near the Oregon border.

Kloster-Gray added that after the tug and barge were seized when they returned to the bay on May 24, it took eight hours for sixty-five agents to access and unload 1,718 burlap sacks of hashish and 1,249 boxes of packaged marijuana from the welded compartments on the barge.

At the conclusion of her opening statement, Kloster-Gray told the jury of eight women and four men that the evidence would support the picture she just outlined and would justify a guilty verdict against Calvin Robinson.

In his opening statement, Calvin Robinson told the jury, "My friends call me Cal."

Federal agents unload and stack the hundreds of boxes of marijuana and bags of hashish from the *Intrepid Venture* and its barge after they were seized in San Francisco Bay on May 24, 1988. *Courtesy of Norman Wood.*

Federal agents survey the boxes of marijuana and bags of hashish on the U.S. Coast Guard dock on Yerba Buena Island, San Francisco Bay. *Courtesy of Norman Wood.*

With those softly spoken words, the hulking man in a brown suit began his campaign to put the government on trial—instead of himself—in one of the biggest drug smuggling cases in U.S. history.

Calvin Robinson, acting as his own lawyer, told the twelve jurors and two alternates, "I am innocent."

Robinson continued, "My son and nephews and I are dredgermen. We are working men on the water. We ran a boat and towed a barge." He also denied that he or his relatives had the "knowledge or aptitude to be an importer or distributor of marijuana."

It soon became clear that Calvin Robinson's trial plan was to attack the government for the charges against him. In a rambling opening statement, he attacked the validity of federal drug laws and transportation regulations and suggested that federal agents had planted the drugs on the barge. He invoked a mysteriously unavailable Seattle company that, Robinson claimed, had contracted with his company, Dredge Masters, for the run that ended in Robinson's arrest.

Robinson stated, "The government's hands were dirty in this case. My hands are clean. This is just one of many cases being played out across this country to justify the government expense for drug interdiction." Robinson blamed "special interest groups" for the indictment returned after federal agents seized his tugboat, the *Intrepid Venture.*

Robinson said the laws under which he was being prosecuted were "lobbied into existence by special interest groups…the Eliot Nesses of the '80s and '90s…Edwin Meese and Commissioner William Von Raab," the former head of U.S. Customs.

Robinson finished his opening statement by claiming that the government had bankrupted him.

"When the government seizes all the money a man has to hire an attorney, the only thing to do is defend oneself or take a court-appointed attorney," Robinson said, explaining to the jury why he was defending himself.

THE PROSECUTION'S CASE

The prosecution has the burden of proving the charges it has alleged. Consequently, with opening statements concluded, the prosecution commenced the presentation of its witnesses first.

Assistant U.S. Attorneys Laurie Kloster-Gray and Matt Pavone intended to take a more deliberate approach to their case. Their plan was to present the jury with facts and just the facts. After Robinson finished his opening statement, they began presenting their evidence. Their first two witnesses were federal agents who testified about the fifty-seven-ton seizure of marijuana and hashish on May 24, 1988.

Federal Drug Enforcement Administration agent Robert Heng testified that the fifty-six tons of marijuana and hashish hidden on Calvin Robinson's barge were worth up to $1 billion on the street. He also testified that the seizure was the largest ever of hashish in U.S. history and a record for a combined hashish-marijuana shipment. He said that the hashish—concentrated marijuana resin—was packaged in bricks, which were wrapped in red cellophane and decorated with gold foil or paint.

Heng further described how the seized marijuana was packaged in vacuum-sealed plastic envelopes with nitrogen injected into them to retard deterioration. Heng also testified that the envelopes were packed in cardboard boxes, which were carefully wrapped in plastic to keep moisture out. The description of the careful packaging of the drugs bolstered the prosecution's position that the defendants were fully aware of the nature and value of their cargo.

Above: U.S. Coast Guard agent Norman Wood (*in foreground*) and other unidentified agents stacking the drugs on the Coast Guard dock. *Courtesy of Norman Wood.*

Opposite: U.S. Coast Guard agent Norman Wood (*right*) and Special Agent Ray Tipton taking a short break on the Coast Guard dock. *Courtesy of Norman Wood.*

The prosecution next presented Norman Wood, the U.S. Customs agent credited with helping break the case.

Wood testified that he received information in early 1987 that Calvin Robinson was planning a drug run in May 1988. Wood said he searched for and located the Robinson worksite: a remote island in Seven Mile Slough, near Rio Vista in Solano County.

During February, March and April 1988, Wood said he staked out the slough, either from a levee road, or by pretending to be a fisherman. He took photographs of Calvin Robinson, his son and his stepson working on the barge and two tugboats—the *Ruby R* and the *Intrepid Venture*—and testified that he saw workers bring cargo containers to the barge, as well as a light industrial crane. This statement was significant: it showed that the defendants were preparing the vessel to take on a large amount of cargo at some point.

Surveillance photo of the tugboats *Intrepid Venture* (*left*) and *Ruby R* alongside a barge with cargo containers in Seven Mile Slough near Isleton in the delta. *Courtesy of Norman Wood.*

Wood also had a court order to place a tracking device aboard the *Intrepid Venture*, but he was unable to do so because starting in early April, someone was aboard the tug day and night. On May 6, the *Intrepid Venture*, with the barge in tow, left San Francisco Bay for the Pacific Ocean.

Though not admissible in evidence, federal agents believed that the Robinsons used the *Ruby R* for a drug run in August 1987. No charges were filed because there was insufficient proof for a prosecution. However, the agents speculated that this August 1987 drug run was successful for the Robinsons. The Robinsons then took their drug profits and gave a certain amount to LendVest officials to run through private accounts and then back to LendVest as "clean money." Some of these drug profits could have also been used to purchase the drugs in the May 1988 drug run. Because this was only speculation and there was no hard evidence, this theory could not be presented to the jury.

The agents further speculated that the *Intrepid Venture* met a mother ship on the high seas 1,200 miles off the coast and took the drugs aboard. However, federal sources said they could not track the *Intrepid Venture* to the mother ship because Agent Wood couldn't sneak the transmitter aboard the tug. Again, this speculation could not be presented to the jury because there was no proof.

Wood said that by posing as a fisherman he was able to watch Calvin Robinson, his son and stepson work on the tug and the one-hundred-foot barge. It was the very same tugboat and barge, Wood testified, that left San Francisco Bay on May 6, 1988, heading for the open sea, and that returned on May 23, loaded with fifty-plus tons of Asian hashish and marijuana.

A significant piece of evidence was presented next. In fact, it was the first physical evidence offered by the prosecution to link Calvin Robinson to the drugs. This evidence was small but powerful. An expert FBI analyst from Washington D.C., Paul Bennett, testified that minute fibers from burlap sacks containing forty-three tons of hashish stowed aboard the *Intrepid Venture* were found on the clothing of Calvin Robinson and his crew. The prosecutor wanted to dispel any notion that Robinson or his crew did not know what was hidden on the barge. The fibers refuted any such testimony by the defense.

Assistant U.S. Attorney Laurie Kloster-Gray questioned several other witnesses, including a marine traffic controller and the owner of a marine supply store. The store owner testified that Calvin Robinson bought sophisticated navigational equipment for his tug *Intrepid Venture*. The prosecution hoped to make the point that it would be unusual for a small tugboat and barge to need such equipment unless it were preparing for a significant journey on the high seas.

Surveillance photo of Calvin Robinson working on the *Intrepid Venture* taken in May 1988 by Norman Wood while he was posing as a fisherman. *Courtesy of Norman Wood.*

A U.S. Coast Guard officer testified that the *Intrepid Venture* reported to marine traffic controllers as it left San Francisco Bay on May 6 that its destination was Eureka. However, Coast Guard lieutenant David Boyd testified that the tugboat's last known location and course was southerly, which, of course, was the opposite direction from Eureka.

At this point, Calvin Robinson requested a continuance of the trial so he could now hire a lawyer. Judge Vukasin denied the request.

Kloster-Gray continued with her prosecution case and called two final prosecution witnesses. One was a handwriting analyst, the other an expert in tug operations.

According to handwriting expert Mary Riker from the U.S. Bureau of Alcohol, Tobacco and Firearms, documents seized from the wheelhouse of the *Intrepid Venture* and from Robinson's briefcase were written by Robinson. One of the documents Riker examined was a stenographer's pad that contained notations on the course of the tug and its barge.

Stan Putzke, who spent thirty-three years in the U.S. Coast Guard and was operations manager for a major Pacific shipping company, testified that the course of the vessels and the construction and use of the barge and tug were unusual and could have been very dangerous. He said the *Intrepid Venture* was a relatively small tug and barely qualified as an oceangoing vessel since it had only a four-day fuel capacity. The deck barge, with its six small cargo containers, couldn't really carry enough cargo to make a trip profitable. Additional fuel tanks were installed in the barge, but their locations were awkward and possibly dangerous, he said. Putzke said if he were transferring cargo in the open sea, he would use a supply ship instead. "It's too dangerous to transfer open cargo on the open sea."

CALVIN ROBINSON PRESENTS HIS DEFENSE

Now it was Robinson's turn to present his defense. His leadoff witnesses provided testimony the jury could use to infer that Robinson and his crew didn't know what they were carrying—and the fifty-six ton seizure on May 24 may not have been marijuana and hashish, as the government claimed.

Robinson presented a drug expert, Loran Anderson, a Florida State University professor. Anderson's testimony cast doubt on the government's identification of the drugs Robinson was accused of smuggling. This testimony was intended to refute the prosecution's forensic chemist, who had testified earlier that laboratory tests showed samples from the shipment were marijuana.

However, Anderson, a botanist, testified there was disagreement whether the government tests identified marijuana or only eliminated the possibility of it being another substance.

On cross-examination by Kloster-Gray, Anderson said he had not tested samples taken from the *Intrepid Venture*'s barge.

Robinson pointed out that during the prosecution's case, Customs agent Norman Wood testified that during an interview following his arrest on May 24, Robinson had told him that he and his crew were contract carriers who did not know what their cargo was.

Wood had also testified Robinson told him the *Intrepid Venture* delivered supplies to survey ships Robinson believed were owned by a company called Seattle Salvage.

In his testimony, Wood said federal investigators had been unable to locate such a company, adding that a company by that name had operated in Seattle in the early 1980s but went out of business in 1985 and never had anything to do with marine operations.

Robinson then presented witness Jan Lamont, the owner of a Seattle telephone answering service. She testified that she took messages for Seattle Salvage in late 1987. Lamont also testified that a man came to her in August of that year and paid cash in advance to take messages for Seattle Salvage. Lamont said this man did not identify himself but said his company was moving to Alaska and needed a telephone number in the Seattle area for a short time. The man also told Lamont that another man would be receiving the messages. Lamont also testified that only about three messages were taken during a three-month period.

Lamont said she did not know whether the messages were picked up and did not have a forwarding address or telephone number for Seattle Salvage.

After the first two defense witnesses were presented, the court recessed for the weekend. The trial would start again the following Tuesday. Robinson informed the judge and prosecutor that he would take the stand himself and would also call his brother Frank Robinson Sr. and his son William Robinson to testify on his behalf. In fact, Calvin Robinson, acting as his own lawyer, had indicated when the trial first started three weeks earlier that he would be taking the witness stand.

However, on Tuesday following the weekend, in a surprise move, Calvin Robinson rested his defense without taking the witness stand to rebut government charges that he smuggled drugs. He also did not call his brother or his son to testify.

This abrupt decision meant that all the testimony was now before the jury. It also meant that after final arguments by the prosecution and defense, and legal instructions by the judge, the case would go to the jury for deliberation.

Though not revealed to the jury, Robinson's decision not to take the witness stand may have been because had he testified, prosecutor Laurie Kloster-Gray could have questioned him about at least part of his extensive criminal background, including convictions in the last ten years on counterfeiting and escape charges.

Closing Arguments

There was a stark contrast between the prosecution's closing argument and that of the defense. The prosecution's case against Calvin Robinson was straightforward and factual. Robinson primarily focused on the theory that he and his crew did not know what their cargo was.

Assistant U.S. Attorney Laurie Kloster-Gray told the jury that she had called twenty-two witnesses, mostly federal agents, who testified that Calvin Robinson skippered the tugboat *Intrepid Venture* and a one-hundred-foot barge into the San Francisco Bay on May 24, 1988. Federal customs and narcotics agents found fifty-six tons of Asian hashish and marijuana aboard the barge.

In his impassioned closing argument, Calvin Robinson repeatedly attacked the validity of federal drug and transportation laws but disputed very few of the prosecution's facts. Instead, he tried to convince the jury that he and his young relatives were contract carriers, working for a Seattle company that had mysteriously disappeared. Robinson claimed it was this unavailable Seattle company that had contracted with his company, Dredge Masters, for the run that ended in his arrest. He also stressed that he and his young crew did not know what their cargo was. He suggested the bust was a setup and the drugs had been planted by federal agents.

After the closing arguments, the judge gave final instructions on the law to the jury. It was time for the case to be given to the jury for deliberation.

THE VERDICT AND THE SENTENCE

Despite Robinson's persuasive-sounding closing argument, after deliberating for less than two hours, the jury found him guilty on all six counts of conspiracy, smuggling and racketeering.

Calvin Robinson, the Napa native who had already spent nineteen of his forty-seven years in prison, now faced a sentence of ten years to life when he came back to court for sentencing by Judge John P. Vukasin. Assistant U.S. Attorney Laurie Kloster-Gray said she would be asking for a life sentence.

Several months after Calvin Robinson was convicted in February 1989, he returned to court for sentencing in June 1989. The sentencing proceedings showcased Calvin Robinson as belligerent to the end.

Before the judge had even delivered the sentence, Robinson menacingly advised Judge John Vukasin, "When you put that chain around my ankle, you'll be putting it around your own neck."

Even at sentencing, Robinson maintained his innocence. "There were no drugs," he shouted. "That's a bunch of malarky. I haven't been engaged in any criminal conduct. I didn't drag my family into this, and I am being persecuted. That is all a bunch of crap."

Robinson also argued that he had been denied an attorney, to which the judge testily responded, "You were offered counsel before trial. You refused counsel....You have no right to pick and choose at this time."

Calvin Robinson. *Courtesy of Norman Wood.*

The prosecutor told the judge that Robinson deserved the maximum because of the "enormity of the drug haul; the fact that he brought eight members of his family into his criminal enterprise; that he has a criminal record going back to his teens; and that he has twice tried to escape from custody."

Judge Vukasin first denied Robinson's request for a new trial and for acquittal, then gave him the maximum prison sentence and fine possible for his role as skipper of the Drug Tug. That sentence was life in prison without parole along with a fine of $4 million for attempting to smuggle fifty-six tons of hashish and marijuana into the United States in May 1988. Along with the stiffest penalty he could give Robinson, the judge stated that Calvin Robinson was a "criminal profiteer" with no redeeming qualities who deserved to be put behind bars for life in the toughest penitentiary the U.S. Bureau of Prisons could find.

6

TRIAL NUMBER TWO

DRUG SMUGGLING CHARGES AGAINST THE CREW

The next trial was the drug smuggling trial against the crew of the *Intrepid Venture*, made up of Calvin Robinson's son William Robinson of Vacaville; Robinson's nephews Frank Robinson of Corning, California, and John Robinson of Santa Rosa, California; and Robinson's stepson Wesley Bastin of Corning. All the crew members were in their early to mid-twenties at the time of trial.

All five men were charged with six counts each of drug smuggling, conspiracy and racketeering.

In its opening statement, the prosecution alleged that after remodeling the barge and the tugboat *Intrepid Venture* (now outfitted with extra fuel tanks), the crew members led by Calvin Robinson set out into the Pacific Ocean on May 6 and met a "mother ship" from which they took on the drug cargo. The prosecution told the jury that it would present evidence of the close family ties between the crew members and Calvin Robinson, as well as other Robinson family members, that would support the charge that they knowingly participated in the conspiracy and attempted to smuggle the contraband into the country.

Deborah DeLambert, lawyer for Calvin Robinson's nephew Frank Robinson Jr., told the jury in her opening statement that convicted drug smuggler Calvin Robinson, the skipper of the Drug Tug, was "reckless, arrogant and inexperienced." She also said that Robinson bullied his son, stepson and the two nephews into working on a three-week sea voyage that ended with their arrest and the seizure of the fifty-six-ton drug cargo the crew was accused of trying to smuggle into the United States.

DeLambert continued her harsh criticism of Calvin Robinson by telling the jury that the young crew was recruited by Calvin, seemingly for a voyage to supply survey ships somewhere in the North Pacific. She called Calvin Robinson "despicable" and said he had "no morals, no conscience." DeLambert told the jury that the evidence would prove that the captain of the *Intrepid Venture* tugboat "intimidated and bullied people who questioned him," and "would not hesitate to use and abuse and then abandon this crew."

DeLambert finished her opening statement by telling the jury that the crewmembers reluctantly agreed to take on the job because other family members asked them to and because they needed the work.

As they had in the first trial against Calvin Robinson, the prosecution opened the March 1989 trial against the crew members by presenting Customs agent Norman Wood. Just as he had in Calvin Robinson's trial, he testified he had posed undercover as a fisherman in the Sacramento River delta to watch members of the Robinson family work on tugboats and a barge.

Wood further testified that he was assigned to investigate an anonymous tip that Calvin Robinson was involved in a marijuana smuggling operation. Wood then said he found Robinson's work area in the Sacramento River delta, at Seven Mile Slough near Isleton in Sacramento County, by following one of the defendants.

In March and April 1988, Wood testified that he maintained surveillance on the tugboat *Ruby R* and a barge that Calvin Robinson and others were working on. Because Wood posed as a fisherman while doing his surveillance, he told the jury, "I did a lot of fishing."

The jury was shown photographs of the work area, the barge, the *Ruby R* and the *Intrepid Venture*. Wood said he placed a court-ordered satellite tracking device aboard the *Ruby R* but was unable to put one on the *Intrepid Venture*. Workers did "extensive" work on the barge, he testified, and put what appeared to be empty cargo containers on its deck.

Federal agents testified that the tugboat was fitted with extra fuel tanks and that hatches had been cut into the cargo compartments, where the drugs were found. Those hatches were later welded shut and painted over at sea to conceal the drugs.

Stanley Putzke, a former member of the U.S. Coast Guard and a shipping consultant, testified for the prosecution that the alterations to the Robinsons' tugboat and barge were not standard in the shipping business. Putzke also testified that it would be "extremely dangerous" to transfer cargo on the high seas.

Welders working to remove the welded hatches from the cargo compartments on the barge following the seizure of the *Intrepid Venture* and the barge. *Courtesy of Norman Wood.*

The prosecution presented other testimony about the events leading up to the drug bust, just as it had done in Calvin's jury. It also presented the same or similar testimony of the actual drug bust in the San Francisco Bay on May 24, 1988, as the other jury heard in Calvin's trial.

Then the government rested its case. It was the defense's turn to present its case to the jury. Just as in Calvin Robinson's jury trial, it became readily apparent that the four crewmembers would deny that they knew what the cargo was and had no part in the alleged conspiracy. However, there was an important twist in the crewmembers' case: it became clear that Calvin Robinson's four young relatives blamed him for misleading them.

The defense called coworkers and family members to testify on behalf of the crew.

The defense elicited testimony acknowledging the existence of the drug shipment, but in their testimony, witnesses maintained the crew members knew nothing of the true intent of the voyage. The defense put all their eggs in that basket, stating the crew members had no knowledge about the drugs.

Bags of hashish were stored next to a fuel tank on the barge. *Courtesy of Norman Wood.*

In fact, the defense presented witnesses who insisted that Calvin Robinson told his crew they were taking food and equipment to two ships.

Closing arguments by the prosecution basically argued that the captain and crew were family members and that they all knew that they were smuggling drugs. The defense countered that the four young men who constituted the members of Calvin Robinson's family were unknowing participants in the drug run of which Robinson, as the captain of the vessels, was the mastermind.

Defense attorney DeLambert told the jury, "It wasn't until late in the trip that they (the crew) noticed things weren't quite right. But then, with Calvin, things were never quite right."

The previous jury took less than two hours to return guilty verdicts on all counts against Calvin Robinson. Reaching a verdict in this second drug smuggling trial—this time against the crewmembers—did not go so quickly. In fact, the jury did not reach a verdict for nearly three days of deliberations. The jury did, however, ultimately reach a verdict on

Agents had to cut into the deck of the barge to access the hidden drugs. *Courtesy of Norman Wood.*

Wednesday, April 12, 1989. The four crewmembers of the Drug Tug were all acquitted of conspiracy and drug smuggling charges.

The defendants' families, who had attended every day of the trial, burst into tears as the court clerk read the "not guilty" verdicts for each of the six felony counts against the four members of the Robinson family.

"We're just glad this is all over," William Robinson, Calvin's son and one of the defendants, said at a post-trial press conference. "It's sad we had to go through this. It was traumatic for our whole family."

William Robinson's codefendants and fellow crewmembers were Calvin's nephews Frank and John Robinson and his stepson Wesley Bastin.

William Robinson's court-appointed lawyer, Henry Wykowski, said, "It was a just verdict. The entire case was based on circumstantial evidence. It was pure speculation that the crew was involved. The jury saw that was the issue."

At the press conference, Wykowski further stated, "Although Calvin [Robinson] may have known about the smuggling operation, his four young relatives did not, and the government was unable to prove any direct links between the crew and the drugs." As an example, by comparison, Wykowski said, "Do you arrest stewardesses if they're working on a plane that brings in cocaine from Colombia?"

The prosecutor, U.S. Attorney Laurie Kloster-Gray, declined comment on the verdict.

This second trial regarding drug smuggling lasted four weeks, after which there were tears of joy and relief. After the jury was excused, the defendants' wives, mothers and aunts hugged.

"We prayed," William Robinson said. "Our family prayed, and our church prayed. Not that we'd get off, but that the right thing would be done....It was a hard year," he said. "My kids were always crying, telling me I was going to prison. We're just glad it's over and we're going back to work."

The verdict in the crewmembers' trial marked the end of the second trial involving the Robinson family. The first trial, against Calvin for drug smuggling, ended in guilty verdicts. The second trial, against the crew for drug smuggling, resulted in acquittals.

7

TRIAL NUMBER THREE

CONSPIRACY AND CURRENCY STRUCTURING CHARGES

The third federal trial would now be the case involving money laundering (specifically, currency structuring reporting violations) and conspiracy against some Robinson family members, some members of the LendVest organization and Robert Pitner of the Joseph Mathews Winery complex. The government dubbed this case the "LendVest" case because it involved LendVest officials and currency structuring through LendVest.

These charges were against David Hanson, former president of LendVest; Robert Pitner, managing general partner of the bankrupt Joseph Mathews Winery complex; Donald Lemmons, a former LendVest vice president and chief appraiser; Sue Lemmons, Don Lemmons's wife and secretary for Dredge Masters Associates; and Diana Rauch Robinson, sister of Sue Lemmons. They would all be tried together.

Diana and Sue's brother Calvin Robinson was also charged in the case along with David Dickson, another former LendVest vice president. Both these men were scheduled for separate trials later in the year.

The charges stemmed from the investigation into the Drug Tug bust, which resulted in the arrest of eleven people and the failure of two Napa businesses, including LendVest. The federal investigation linked the captain of the tugboat pulling the barge, former Napa resident Calvin Robinson, and members of his family to LendVest executive officers.

The federal agents charged that the officials running LendVest at the time violated federal currency laws in the attempt to conceal a $200,000 transaction with cash from an alleged earlier drug deal involving the defendants in the May 1988 Drug Tug seizure.

Following an investigation into LendVest, a federal grand jury issued the indictments on charges of conspiracy and violating currency transactions laws against the former officers of LendVest, their business associates and members of the Robinson family.

The federal government did not charge the defendants in the LendVest case with money laundering because it would have had difficulty proving that the money was from an illegal source. The prosecution believed that it was but had no legally admissible proof that the money was traced to an illegal source. Consequently, the government charged currency structuring. This was a relatively new federal statute prohibiting the breaking up of large cash deposits into smaller amounts to avoid IRS depositing requirements. There was no requirement to show the illegal source of the money. In fact, the trial judge ruled that there would be no mention of the alleged source of the money during the trial.

This freed the prosecution to focus on demonstrating that the defendants had knowingly and willfully conspired to evade IRS reporting requirements by breaking up the Robinson funds into smaller amounts and funneling it through their personal checking accounts into LendVest. The government had testimony that David Hanson, at least, was aware of federal reporting regulations when the deposits were made and that there had been discussions among LendVest officers about how to arrange the deposits of the $200,000. Without having to prove the source of the funds was derived from an illegal source, it appeared that the case against Hanson, and perhaps some of the other LendVest officers, was strong.

OPENING STATEMENTS

This federal trial took place in April 1989. In opening statements, the prosecution attorney for the government said they would not focus on the source of the money but rather on what the defendants did with the cash. They would center on bank documents and business associations, not family relationships, and that their case would be a straightforward criminal case against the defendants.

The prosecution, through Assistant U.S. Attorney Eric Swenson, said the government had volumes of bank documents and piles of new $100

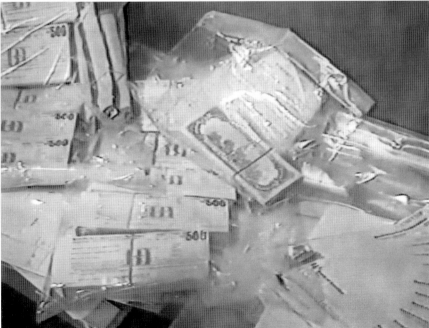

Bundles of cash and other bank documents seized in the federal case against David Hanson and others for currency structuring and conspiracy. *Courtesy of KTVU Fox Channel 2.*

bills to show that the defendants conspired to hide large cash transactions from the IRS.

However, a not-so-subtle pattern emerged in the opening statements for the defense. As in the prior trial against the tugboat crew for drug smuggling, the defense put the blame on Calvin Robinson. The current trial for violation of currency structuring was no different: Calvin Robinson was blamed.

In their opening statements to the jury, defense attorneys said it was misplaced trust in Calvin Robinson that led members of his family and their business associates at LendVest Mortgage Inc. into the alleged money laundering scheme that had rocked Napa County the previous year. The defense attorneys did not dispute the existence of the money or the accuracy of the bank records, but they said they would show that federal authorities were wrong in their interpretation of the defendants' actions.

Don Tamborello, the lawyer representing defendant Sue Lemmons, Robinson's sister and the wife of former LendVest chief appraiser and former vice president Don Lemmons, said, "Calvin Robinson was the bad apple…the bad seed of the Robinson family."

During opening statements, the defense lawyers insinuated that their clients were duped by Calvin Robinson about the source of the hundreds of thousands of dollars that came into the Robinson businesses. The lawyers stated that the defendants thought they were just helping members of their family, including Calvin Robinson, by routing the cash through their personal checking accounts and back into the now-bankrupt LendVest Mortgage Company.

The defense lawyers further told the jury that either Calvin Robinson refused to tell them the source of the money, or he told them it was cash payment for large dredging jobs.

Robert Pitner's attorney, John Milano, stated that there was virtually no testimony in the prosecution's case about his client. Only three of the prosecution witnesses mentioned Pitner's name, noting his alleged involvement in a cash banking transaction on November 25, 1987, which included the defendants and several other LendVest employees who had not been charged.

Attorneys for Diana Robinson Rauch told the jury that Calvin Robinson took advantage of Diana's poor health when he convinced his youngest sister to go into business with him. In that partnership, Calvin Robinson instructed Rauch how to set up bookkeeping procedures and make the banking deposits that eventually led to the charges in this case.

Other defense lawyers said in their opening statements that Calvin Robinson, already convicted of drug smuggling and scheduled to be tried on currency structuring separately from the other five defendants, lied to their clients about the source of the currency they were accused of funneling through their personal and business checking accounts during the fall of 1987 and winter of 1987–88.

With opening statements by the lawyers on both sides concluded, presentation of witnesses in the currency structuring violation charges against Hanson and other defendants began.

The Prosecution's Case

In a methodical manner, the prosecution presented evidence that on November 24, 1987, Sue Lemmons and Dianna Robinson Rauch gave David Hanson $200,000 in sequentially numbered, uncirculated $100 bills. The following day, Hanson asked several people, including the defendants in this case, as well as other LendVest employees, to deposit the cash in their personal checking accounts and then write checks back to LendVest.

Bank documents presented to the jury showed that all the deposits were in amounts of less than $10,000, so no IRS currency transaction reports were generated. But according to the prosecution's first witness, Deborah Waterdown, a supervisor at the North Napa branch of Bank of America, the fact that the cash was brand new, and the serial numbers were in sequence, made bank officials suspicious. Waterdown testified to the jury that it is rare for depositors to bring in such quantities of brand-new bills.

Some tellers at that branch office recognized the depositors as employees of LendVest mortgage and told Waterdown about the deposits. Waterdown testified that she reported the deposits to Bank of America officials, who, in turn, contacted the IRS agents already investigating the Robinson family business.

Assistant U.S. Attorney Eric Swenson called the former corporate secretary for Dredge Masters Associates, Debra Jackson. Jackson told the jury that she had worked at the Dredge Masters office in Southern California, handling corporate business matters. She testified that Dredge Masters records showed that the company did more than twenty dredging jobs in 1987, including one in Hilo, Hawaii, during August of that year. Calvin Robinson handled that job, she testified, and added that Sue

Lemmons had told her that the payment for the work—$235,000—was made in cash. The Hilo job was said to be a dredging project, but the prosecution hoped the jury would infer it was a marijuana smuggling operation.

The prosecution also presented Christopher Padley, a former LendVest vice president. He testified that LendVest was in financial trouble and that as early as December 1987, employees prayed about the company's financial troubles and lack of capital during weekly prayer meetings.

Padley testified about a November 1987 business transaction that was the core of the prosecution's allegations against the defendants. He told the jury that on November 25, 1987, he deposited two bundles of currency into his personal checking accounts at the request of David Hanson. Padley then remitted the amount to LendVest with two personal checks. He also testified that Hanson asked him how many checking accounts he had and instructed him to deposit the bundles in separate accounts to avoid "the hassle of standing there while they count it out."

Padley further testified that he did not question Hanson about the transaction, nor did he know at the time that it is illegal to arrange currency transactions to avoid the reporting requirements. He also testified that it was his understanding that the currency was part of a larger amount that Calvin Robinson invested in LendVest.

Padley told the court that he resigned from the company in mid-May because he was worried about its financial stability.

Also testifying for the prosecution was Joan Nunley, a Napa Valley Bank manager. She said that Diana Robinson Rauch told her just after the account was opened that Rauch had won three medical malpractice suits and would be receiving weekly cash disbursements from her lawyer.

Nunley said she told Rauch that any currency deposits in excess of $10,000 would be reported to the IRS, regardless of the source. Nunley also testified that Rauch deposited cash in the account fifteen or twenty times over a two-month period.

Nunley was the last in a parade of tellers and officials from several Napa banks who testified to scores of deposits in the fall and winter of 1987–88. They said the deposits were typically about $5,000 in new, sequentially numbered $100 bills, they said.

Other witnesses told different stories about what David Hanson told them about the large amount of cash that came into LendVest. Several witnesses testified that Hanson confirmed to them the cash invested in LendVest on November 25, 1987, was, in fact, part of a medical malpractice suit won by Diana Robinson Rauch.

But witness Andrea Langley, who worked as a bookkeeper for LendVest, testified that Hanson told her the money came from Calvin Robinson, who, Hanson said, had a dredging job so big it was "comparable to building the Panama Canal."

Witness testimony indicated that Hanson received $200,000 cash on November 24, 1987, brought into the company by Don Lemmons, then chief appraiser for LendVest. According to witnesses, the following day Hanson asked several LendVest employees to deposit some of the cash into their personal checking accounts and remit it back to LendVest by writing a check.

Langley testified that Hanson knew that currency deposits of more than $10,000 are reported to the IRS. She told the jury that sometime before the November 25 transaction, Hanson asked her how much could be deposited without being reported to the IRS. She testified that she told Hanson about the $10,000 limit. Langley also said she did not question Hanson when he told her to help count the $200,000 in new $100 bills, or when she deposited $9,500 in her checking account and wrote a check to LendVest for $10,000.

Clearly, the prosecution had presented witnesses who were able to impeach Hanson's credibility by testifying about the different stories Hanson told others about where the $200,000 cash came from, as well as his knowledge of what constituted currency structuring and what is reportable to the IRS by law.

Other prosecution witnesses testified that Sue Robinson Lemmons withdrew $192,000 from a Dredge Masters Associates account, put the money in a brown paper grocery bag and gave it to Sandra Hanson, wife of David Hanson.

Sue Lemmons made that withdrawal, comprising $160,000 in blank traveler's checks and money orders and a $32,000 cashier's check to David Hanson, on the same day the *Intrepid Venture* was due back from its ocean voyage—May 24, 1988.

John McDonald of Napa said that he had been a friend of Hanson and his wife, Sandra, for about twelve years. He testified that Sandra brought the paper grocery bag to his house on the evening of May 24 and asked him to keep it for her. He said he did not ask what was in the bag or look inside it. He testified he put the bag in his closet. He thought it was a birthday present or a surprise of some sort.

The next day, McDonald testified, David Hanson called McDonald and asked him to bring the bag to the LendVest offices in Napa. Special Agent Christopher Cooley of the IRS testified that it was at the LendVest offices that the IRS, who knew about the $32,000 cashier's check payable to Hanson, seized the grocery bag and money from Hanson.

The jury also heard testimony about cash hidden in a laundry hamper. Special Agent Cooley told the court he was with the team of agents who twice searched the Lemmons residence on Olive Hill Lane in Napa. During the second search, on June 3, 1988, Cooley found $13,180 in cash in a laundry hamper in the Lemmons house. Cooley said he had looked in the hamper during the first search, on May 24, but the money was not there at that time.

IRS agent Roger Sheilds testified that he interviewed Hanson on May 25, 1988. When he asked Hanson about the $200,000 in cash that was funneled into LendVest on November 25, 1987, through the personal checking accounts of the company's employees and associates, Hanson told Sheilds that the disbursements—all less than $10,000—were loans.

Sheilds said that when asked, Hanson admitted the recipients of the cash never asked for the loans. Everyone who received cash from Hanson wrote checks back to LendVest for the same amount on November 25. Sheilds also testified that Hanson told him he knew about the federal statute that requires banks to report all currency transactions over $10,000.

Perhaps the key testimony against Hanson came from David Dickson and from other former LendVest employees who testified that Hanson was fully aware of federal reporting regulations when the deposits were made and that there had been some discussion among LendVest officers about how to arrange the deposits of the $200,000.

U.S. Attorney Eric Swenson used his last prosecution witness to tie together previous testimony about the financial records, which formed the basis of the case against David Hanson and the other defendants charged with conspiracy and currency structuring. The testimony was about the flow of cash through Napa bank accounts controlled by the defendants.

Michael Hagstrom, a special agent with the IRS, provided jurors with a summary of currency transactions allegedly made by some of the defendants in late 1987. Hagstrom testified that bank records showed several of the defendants made almost daily deposits of currency—mostly new $100 bills—into bank accounts for Calvin Robinson, Dredge Masters Associates, the Robinson family business and a company simply called "Robinson."

The government alleged those deposits, mostly in amounts of $5,000, totaled more than $750,000 and showed a conspiracy on the part of some of the defendants to hide the cash flow from the IRS.

The prosecution rested its case confident that it had presented the jury with ample evidence of conspiracy and currency structuring—the breaking up of large amounts of cash into smaller deposits to avoid IRS reporting requirements.

The Defense Presents Its Case

It was now time for the defense to present its case. The plan was to not contest many of the facts in the case, or the accuracy of the tons of cash, legal papers and bank documents presented as evidence. The plan was to maintain that all the transactions were legitimate business dealings and blame Calvin Robinson.

Against the prosecution's ample testimony, bank records and seized cash, the defense sought to raise doubt about the defendants' knowledge and intentions. The defendants presented a joint defense that only Calvin Robinson knew the real source of the money. The defense lawyers painted Hanson, Pitner, the Lemmonses and Diana Robinson Rauch as victims of Calvin Robinson's deceit and, in the case of Diana Robinson Rauch, even Calvin's threats.

The defense, composed of six court-appointed attorneys, hoped to convince jurors that if there was a conspiracy it was between Calvin Robinson and unknown persons, not their clients.

The defense lawyers hoped to prove that because of love and loyalty and the firm belief that Calvin Robinson, who had spent nineteen of his forty-seven years in prison, had gone straight, Diana Robinson Rauch and Sue Lemmons were eager to help their brother in his efforts to start a new dredging business. The defense intended to show that the scores of cash transactions made by the defendants at Calvin's direction were due to their misguided trust in their brother.

The joint defense plan was to show that loyalty led the Robinson family astray when the alleged drug smuggling and money laundering scandal broke in May 1988.

When Diana Robinson Rauch took the witness stand, she testified about a disabling illness from which she suffered and her personal and business relations with her older brother Calvin Robinson. Rauch told the jury that she suffered severe gastrointestinal damage because of an illness several years prior. Since that time, she had been in constant pain and had taken prescription medication. According to testimony by Rauch and Richard Thorson, the

Napa pharmacist who had filled Rauch's prescriptions for years, these drugs included tranquilizers, sleeping pills, antibiotics and antispasmodics. Rauch testified that those drugs often caused her to be confused and tired.

Rauch told the jury that she was given about $1 million in bearer bonds and that she had been threatened against revealing the source of the bonds. She further testified that her brother Calvin Robinson told her she "would get hurt" if she ever told anyone who gave them the bonds, issued by Banque Nationale de Paris of Luxembourg. But Rauch told the jury that the negotiable bonds, similar to cashier's checks, came from William Lyttle, a Robinson family cousin. Rauch also testified that Calvin told her the money was an advance on a multimillion-dollar gold dredging job in Colombia that Lyttle was helping set up with an English mining company. The bearer bonds, in denominations ranging from $100,000 to $250,000, were distributed to some of the defendants. The prosecution maintained that the bearer bonds and almost $1 million in currency were profits from the alleged August 1987 drug run. The defense was equally adamant that the defendants knew nothing of the source of the money and that Calvin Robinson had lied to his family.

Because the defendants in this third federal trial were charged only with currency structuring and not with any drug-related violations, the prosecution did not have to prove the structured money came from any illegal source, and in fact, the judge had ruled that the prosecution was not allowed to make any references to drug smuggling.

As a result, the jurors in this third federal case heard no mention of the May 24, 1988 seizure of the Robinson tugboat and its barge, in which narcotics agents had found more than fifty-six tons of hashish and marijuana.

Further, the jury, by the judge's order, was not aware of Calvin Robinson's conviction in his recent trial on conspiracy and drug smuggling charges resulting from the May tugboat seizure.

The defense also presented character witnesses for Don and Sue Lemmons. Harlen Smetzer Jr. and his wife, Linda, testified that she and her husband were good friends of the Lemmonses through their mutual school and church involvement. Dr. William Wiley, a Napa physician and his wife, Marianne, also testified to the Lemmonses' reputation as generous, hardworking and upright community members.

David Hanson took the witness stand in his own defense and, referring to a $200,000 cash investment in LendVest in November 1987, testified to the jury, "I had no idea it was illegal, and if I'd known, I would never have done it."

It was this investment, which was funneled into LendVest through employees' personal checking accounts, that was at the core of the prosecution's case against Hanson and the other defendants in this case as to the conspiracy and currency structuring charges.

In his testimony, Hanson asserted that he was ignorant of the 1986 federal law that makes it a crime to break up large amounts of cash into smaller deposits to avoid IRS reporting requirements. Hanson told the jury that he never tried to hide records of the transaction and cooperated with IRS agents investigating the case.

In fact, Hanson contradicted the testimony of several former LendVest employees who testified as prosecution witnesses, that LendVest was in financial trouble months before it collapsed in the wake of the Drug Tug smuggling and money laundering scandal.

Hanson told the jury that the LendVest employees were mistaken when they testified that he told them conflicting stories about the source of the $200,000.

Under direct examination by his lawyer, Hanson testified that he did not really know the source of the $200,000 in new $100 bills—only that codefendant Sue Lemmons brought the cash to him and asked that the investment remain confidential. He said that was why he divided the cash into amounts of less than $10,000, gave it to employees and some business associates to deposit in their personal checking accounts and had them remit the money in checks to LendVest, all on one day.

However, on cross-examination, Assistant U.S. Attorney Eric Swenson informed Hanson that if the proper paperwork was filed, confidentiality of the investor would not be preserved. Hanson admitted that he knew he would have to file other IRS tax forms that would identify the investor and that approximately eleven people at LendVest knew about the investment.

"So, in what way was that confidential?" Swenson asked Hanson. After a pregnant pause from Hanson, Swenson rephrased the question and asked, "Dividing the cash into amounts of less than $10,000—how did that make the investment confidential?" After another long pause, Hanson replied, "I don't know how to answer that." Hanson's defense, as with at least two of his codefendants, was that he did not know it was illegal to arrange the investment in that way.

Clearly attorney Swenson had caught Hanson in a substantial contradiction. This was significant because the government must prove that Hanson and the other defendants knowingly and willingly violated the currency structuring law—part of the Money Laundering Act of 1986.

In the end, Robert Pitner presented no evidence on his behalf because he thought it was unnecessary. His attorney, John Milano, told the court he would not call any witnesses or offer any evidence in his client's defense. The reason for this decision by Milano may have been because of an earlier ruling by Judge Vukasin—that the prosecution would not be allowed to present any evidence of the business associations between LendVest and Joseph Mathews Winery complex, of which Pitner had been the managing general partner. As a result, there had been virtually no evidence offered nor any mention of Pitner in the prosecution's case.

Defense attorneys wrapped up their defense by presenting as witnesses some Napa residents who testified about their investments in LendVest, which was now in bankruptcy. These witnesses stated that they believed David Hansen and others at LendVest were trustworthy people. They did not think that any fault lay with LendVest. They felt that, but for the media splash when the drug bust occurred, there would not have been a run on the company and things would have been sorted out.

It was time for closing arguments.

Closing Arguments

As the seven-week trial neared its end, dozens of Napans turned out to show support for defendants in the LendVest criminal trial. The spectators were mostly church and school friends of defendants Don and Sue Lemmons, who filled one side of the federal courtroom to hear the attorneys summarize and argue the complicated money laundering case.

The prosecution, through U.S. Attorney Eric Swenson, went first. Swenson showed the jury large orange and green charts, detailing the flow of cash that was the heart of the government's case. He argued that the motive behind the complicated, if not sophisticated, alleged money laundering operation was "greed, one of the basest instincts of mankind." He then showed jurors a copy of the twenty-page federal grand jury indictment, which charged the defendants with various counts of conspiracy and currency structuring.

Swenson alleged that the evidence showed that some of the defendants made almost daily deposits of cash into business and personal checking accounts in Napa banks during the fall and winter of 1987–88, in amounts of less than $10,000 to avoid having the bank file an IRS currency transaction report.

The prosecution also alleged that the defendants were involved in a cash transaction on November 24, 1987, in which $200,000 was funneled into LendVest Mortgage Inc., through the personal checking accounts of some of the defendants and several LendVest employees. Most of the currency was in new, uncirculated $100 bills.

The difficulty for the prosecution was that the government believed that the $200,000 was prior drug smuggling profits from August 1987, which resulted in the funneling of cash on November 24, 1987. This belief by the prosecution was only that—a belief. The lawyers could not prove it beyond a reasonable doubt. They could not present any evidence of this belief.

While it was true that the prosecution did not have to prove the source of the money was from an illegal activity, the case was possibly more difficult to prove without a drug smuggling connection to the money laundering case to convince jurors that there was some illicit motive behind the structuring of the currency. To the jury, it might appear to be just a technical violation of the law. As a result, the government needed to convince the jurors that the defendants knowingly and willingly broke the law in avoiding IRS notification of the deposits.

Prosecuting attorney Eric Swenson dumped a sack of crisp, new $100 bills onto the table in front of him and appealed to the jurors' common sense in determining the facts of the case and the defendants' motives.

The defense attorneys argued that the currency structuring law was so new that even bank employees who testified as prosecution witnesses did not know what the reporting requirements were.

Tony Tamborello, Sue Lemmons's attorney, argued that Sue Lemmons and her sister Diana Rauch were tricked by their brother Calvin Robinson. Tamborello told the jury that Sue Lemmons believed Calvin when he told her the cash was payment for a dredging job in Hilo, Hawaii, and when she deposited it in $5,000 increments, she was only following Calvin's instructions.

Tamborello went even further and said that everyone in the Robinson family, particularly Sue Lemmons, wanted to believe Calvin—an ex-con who, by the time of this trial, had spent twenty of his forty-eight years in prison—had gone straight and was running a successful legitimate business venture.

John Milano, attorney for Pitner, kept his argument brief. He reminded the jury that there had been virtually no direct evidence against his client. No witnesses or evidence were presented by Milano on behalf of his client's defense. Milano told the jury, "It's the bottom of the ninth inning and you're ahead. You don't even have to go to bat."

David Hanson was represented by his court-appointed attorney, James Larson. He told the jury, in his closing argument, that his client's actions—which led to indictment on seven counts of conspiracy and currency structuring—were mistakes, not craft or trickery. "You can believe that David Hanson is a complete fool," Larson said, "or that he is naive. But that does not make him guilty."

Larson argued that Hanson trusted codefendant Sue Lemmons, who in turn had misplaced her trust in her brother Calvin Robinson.

As to the funneling of $200,000 cash investment into LendVest in November 1987 through the personal checking accounts of some of the defendants and several LendVest employees, Larson argued that Hanson had no idea he was acting illegally when he funneled this large sum.

As to the specific conspiracy charge, Larson argued, "The conspiracy charge against Hanson was a 'sloppy' catch-all charge. Conspiracy is a sloppy concept that encourages sloppy thinking."

Then James Larson concluded his closing argument on behalf of David Hanson in dramatic fashion. "The display of numerous bank records and hundreds of dollars in new, sequentially numbered hundred-dollar bills was just a distraction by the government." Waiving a rubber trout around the courtroom, he told the jurors that the government's tactics were "red herrings."

With the closing arguments concluded by the defense, the prosecution had one more turn to give a rebuttal argument to the defense's closing.

Assistant U.S. Attorney Eric Swenson said that the evidence showed that Hanson and the other four defendants knew they were breaking the law in trying to hide a total of $775,000 from IRS by laundering it through personal checking accounts and LendVest. "You don't lie when you're innocent," Swenson said. "It's the natural inclination of human beings to put cash in the bank. It's the natural inclination of a businessman to put cash in the bank—not spread it out over three months, not divide it up into twenty different transactions."

Swenson told the jury, "It is illogical to think the defendants would continue the pattern of suspicious financial transactions for nine months if they thought it was a legitimate and normal way to do business."

The arguments were then finished, and Judge Vukasin instructed the jury on the law as it applied to the charges. The case was then handed over to the jury to commence deliberations.

THE VERDICTS

The trial on the conspiracy and currency structuring violations was estimated to last four weeks, but six weeks had elapsed; now the jury was deliberating, considering a total of twenty-one counts of conspiracy and currency structuring against the five defendants: Diana Robinson Rauch; her sister Sue Lemmons; Sue's husband, Don Lemmons; David Hanson; and Robert Pitner.

After a long period of deliberation in the complicated financial case, the equally complicated verdict left both sides claiming small victories and most of the defendants in a state of subdued relief.

The federal jury deadlocked on all the conspiracy charges. However, they convicted David Hanson on four counts and Robert Pitner on one count of currency structuring. Hanson received a four-and-a-half-year sentence in federal prison, and Pitner received only probation. Based on the evidence presented in court, the judge found the culpability of these two men was different.

Don Lemmons was acquitted of all charges. Diana Robinson Rauch was acquitted on all charges except the deadlocked count of conspiracy. The jury deadlocked on currency structuring and conspiracy charges against Sue Lemmons.

Immediately after the verdict, U.S. Attorney Eric Swenson said he would ask for a new trial on all the deadlocked charges. Eventually, however, after negotiations with Diana Robinson Rauch's attorney, she pleaded guilty to one count of currency structuring to avoid retrial on the conspiracy charge and received a sentence of five years' probation. Sue Lemmons did the same as her sister Diana, and she also received the same sentence of five years' probation.

The prosecution eventually dropped the conspiracy charges and structuring case against Dave Dickson.

As to Calvin Robinson's currency structuring and conspiracy case, which had been severed from that of the other defendants, the intent of the prosecution was to try him separately after the other defendants. Eventually, however, because Calvin Robinson had previously received the maximum sentence in the drug smuggling case—life in prison—the prosecution decided not to pursue the additional charges of currency structuring and conspiracy.

There remained the state fraud case facing Hanson as well as Pitner.

The scene leading to the state fraud case can be summarized as follows: the federal drug smuggling case against Calvin Robinson had concluded with a conviction. His tugboat crew was acquitted of drug smuggling in federal court. As for the currency structuring case, it resulted in four convictions as to Hanson and one count as to Pitner. Hanson eventually received four and a half years in federal prison. Pitner received five months' probation. Some of the other defendants in the currency structuring case were convicted but lightly sentenced to probation. No one was convicted of the conspiracy charges.

During this time, there were also some civil suits filed against LendVest. The attorney for many of the creditors who filed suit was Steve Linthicum, a lawyer from Sonoma. These suits against LendVest settled in June 1991 without a trial.

Further, during the time that federal drug smuggling trials and the currency structuring trials were occurring, the bankruptcy proceedings for LendVest Mortgage Inc., which were now under the eye of newly appointed bankruptcy trustee Charles Sims of Napa, were also taking place. Sims had replaced Charles Duck after it was discovered he was embezzling from some of the bankruptcy cases he was overseeing.

Sims was now in the process of contacting LendVest's investors and creditors, as well as marshaling whatever assets remained of the once prosperous and fast-growing Napa-based mortgage company.

For the creditors, the best thing that happened in the bankruptcy proceedings was getting a trustee (Sims) with whom they could work, was honest and who was completely devoted to their best interests. A bankruptcy trustee often needs legal representation. Sims hired the highly regarded Santa Rosa bankruptcy law firm of Geary, Shea, O'Donnell & Grattan. From that firm, attorney Steven M. Olsen was assigned to represent Sims in his effort to return as much of the creditors' investments as possible.

Under his competent watch, Sims found solvent and potentially liable defendants in the accounting firms of Grant & Ganze and KMG Main-Hurdman, both of which had been associated with Harvey Grant between 1983 and 1988. However, despite Sims's valiant efforts, there were still hundreds of people who had lost millions of dollars in the LendVest scandal.

Bankruptcy trustee Chuck Sims's attorney, Steven M. Olsen, later stated that the trustee was ultimately able to return approximately $300,000 to the unsecured creditor class. This sum, according to Olsen, amounted to approximately 18 cents on the dollar to the unsecured creditors. The final decree, which approved the plan of distribution to the creditors, did not occur until September 1, 1995.

It was under these background circumstances that the state fraud case against David Hanson began.

PART II

THE LENDVEST FRAUD CASE

8

WHO WAS DAVID HANSON?

For many years, Napa mortgage loan officer David Hanson worked for other people. His longtime employer was Leo Lieberman, and although Hanson had acquired a real estate license in 1964, he was never active in real estate sales. However, he dreamed of owning his own business, becoming his own boss. He had good ideas and was convinced he could be successful.

In 1981, Hanson opened his own mortgage company, Napa Valley Mortgage. He owned and operated the company himself, employing only two, and later three, employees. Napa Valley Mortgage brokered conventional, FHA and VA real estate loans. In addition, it also solicited cash investments from private investors and either paid interest on the accounts or offered deeds of trust in exchange.

Napa Valley Mortgage expanded during the 1980s, ultimately opening branches in five California cities, and by 1987, the firm employed more than seventy people. The name was then changed to LendVest Mortgage Inc. By the late 1980s, Hanson boasted that LendVest was the fastest-growing mortgage company in California. During this time, Hanson maintained a lavish lifestyle, earning an annual salary in excess of $300,000 and drawing on a significant expense account. His personal appearance reflected his success: he wore tailored sport coats with linen slacks, silk shirts and Italian leather shoes and was well-groomed. He lived in a large, well-appointed home, drove a Porsche and threw extravagant parties for employees and investors.

This property at 1991 Pine Street in Napa was the former home of David Hanson. *Photo by the author.*

Hanson was seen as an upstanding citizen, an active member of Napa's First Baptist Church who held prayer meetings at his mortgage company and described himself as "a good Christian person." He even convinced several church members to invest in LendVest. He worked hard to achieve

Formerly the First Baptist Church in Napa, it is now called Crosswalk Church. *Photo by the author.*

his ambition. He was a highly regarded member of the Napa community, respected by church members and earned the praise of his peers in business.

But ultimately, Hanson became addicted to his success—the beautiful home, the Porsche, the lavish holiday parties, his reputation as an influential community member—and he would do anything to maintain it. So, when his business faltered, he was desperate to raise money to keep from going under.

Hanson began to sell company stock to employees and individual investors, and he misrepresented the company's financial status. He also agreed to repurchase some investors' stocks upon request, but he failed to do so. As a result, most investors lost their entire investment. At some point, Hanson no longer owned 100 percent of the company's stock, but he made sure he retained exclusive control over the management of company affairs. The acts he committed were not creative or imaginative; they were criminal. And the damage to the citizens of Napa was real and profoundly harmful.

Hanson knew certified public accountant Harvey Grant, who owned an extremely successful accounting firm. Grant was well known in the Napa Valley. He often spoke at Napa Chamber of Commerce and local business organization functions regarding legislation affecting taxes and its effect on the consumer/taxpayer.

In 1982, Hanson hired Grant to handle all accounting for LendVest. The firm remained solvent until 1983. In 1983–84, because of Hanson's extravagant lifestyle, LendVest began to lose money at a rapid rate. When Grant prepared the annual financial statement for the 1983–84 fiscal year, the figures revealed a negative net worth. He knew this financial insolvency would jeopardize various lines of credit with LendVest's banks and would threaten VA and FHA approval for brokering loans, so he inserted a "going concern disclaimer" in the financial statement. This disclaimer was an indication that LendVest might be unable to remain financially viable through the next year.

Certified public accountant Harvey Grant. *Courtesy of Napa County Historical Society.*

Grant personally delivered this financial statement, and when Hanson saw the "going concern disclaimer" he was distressed. He told Grant that if he showed that financial statement to anyone, his company would be out of business. Hanson then asked Grant to prepare a fictitious financial statement showing a profitable operation in compliance with all the various government and banking requirements.

At first, Grant did not want to prepare such a statement. He had known Hanson for many years and believed him to be a good Christian who meant well, but when he examined the LendVest books, he saw that Hanson was deceiving people. However, he believed Hanson intended to make things right with his clients and employees and that in time he would again be successful.

Hanson was confident, charismatic and persuasive. He exuded honesty. So, Grant reluctantly agreed to prepare the false financial statement. From then on, at Hanson's request, Grant prepared two sets of financial statements for the company. From 1983 through May 1988, when LendVest closed, the company was insolvent. The true financial statements reflected large losses and a growing negative net worth, but the false financial statements always showed a fiscally healthy, profitable company with a large positive net worth.

These false financial statements were used to obtain Department of Real Estate (DRE) permits, FHA approvals, VA approvals and extensive lines of credit with various financial institutions. The DRE securities permit enabled LendVest to guarantee payment to private investors who purchased trust deeds.

Despite its large losses, Hanson was able to keep his company afloat only because he successfully convinced dozens of people to invest large sums of money in his company in return for unsecured (not guaranteed by any collateral) promissory notes using the false financial statements and misrepresenting the company's financial status to secure investments.

Hanson offered an attractive feature for investors in the higher interest rates he paid. Word of these rates spread, and investors flocked to his door. Hanson was always careful to ensure that his investors received their monthly interest payments in a timely manner. However, whenever an investor would ask for their principal back, Hanson convinced them such a withdrawal was unwise.

He also employed other illegal means to keep his insolvent company going. He encouraged investors to sign a power of attorney, telling them it would be used only for their protection in processing the paperwork. With the investment paperwork kept in-house, Hanson explained, there would be no delay or loss of the documents, and the transaction would go smoothly.

However, what Hanson told the investor and what was done with the client's power of attorney were two different things. Hanson used the power of attorney to assign the investor's trust deed to another investor for more money without the original investor's knowledge. He also used investors' power of attorney to substitute unsecured, interest-only promissory notes in place of deeds of trust underlying customers' loans. Additionally, when a person borrowed money from LendVest in exchange for a trust deed, Hanson would assign that trust deed to Capitol Thrift, which then funded the loan, and he would subsequently sell the same trust deed to another, unsuspecting investor. This second trust deed assignment was never recorded.

Hanson also controlled another company, Napa Valley Distributing, and he funneled over $1 million from LendVest into this firm. In the mid-1980s, he also began investing money from LendVest in Joseph Mathews Winery, another company in which he owned a controlling interest. In fact, Hanson was the main source of income for Joseph Mathews Winery. His accountant, Grant, later said that LendVest funneled hundreds of thousands of dollars into the winery and that Hanson also convinced numerous people to invest directly in the winery and become limited partners.

Both Napa Valley Distributing and the winery lost money. In January 1987, the winery accountant advised the company to file for bankruptcy.

In 1988, Hanson became increasingly desperate for cash, and he sought investors for a new limited partnership called LendVest Mortgage II (LendVest II). However, the money that investors invested in LendVest II actually went into the coffers of Napa Valley Distributing and Joseph Mathews Winery.

The bubble burst in May 1988, when a tugboat seized in San Francisco Bay was found to be carrying millions of dollars of illegal drugs. Eventually it became known that Hanson and Robert Pitner (a partner in Joseph Mathews Winery) were involved in money laundering activities with the drug smuggling defendants who were transporting the drugs. Local, state and federal agencies immediately descended on LendVest, and their investigation revealed the fraudulent means by which Hanson was keeping his company afloat.

In the spring of 1988, both LendVest and the winery declared bankruptcy. LendVest owed its investors $7.9 million.

9

THE CRIME REPORTS GO TO THE NAPA COUNTY DISTRICT ATTORNEY

Reports from the myriad local, state and federal agencies involved in the investigation of LendVest were sent to the Napa County District Attorney's Office. The district attorney at that time was Jerome Mautner, who had been Napa County district attorney since 1983.

As district attorney, Jerome Mautner was hardworking and conscientious. He had an impressive knowledge of the law, and he often took a hardline approach in charging suspects. Typically, when the police submit a crime report, the district attorney gives the case a general overview and assigns a deputy to review the file in detail and make a recommendation as to whether a criminal complaint should be filed.

In the LendVest case, Mautner knew from his initial review of the police reports that this case was significant in terms of the financial devastation to people in the community. He also knew there might be numerous conflicts of interest in his office that could potentially impact the prosecution's case. A conflict of interest occurs when an individual's personal interests—family, friendships, financial or social factors—could compromise their judgment, decisions or actions. A prosecutor has a duty to zealously represent the interests of the people of the State of California. If that prosecutor has a personal relationship to either a victim or the defendant, it could affect their professional objectivity.

Mautner was termed a "working district attorney," which meant that he had to carry a caseload besides being the chief office administrator. His staff was small, and because of the large number of victims from the LendVest scandal, there would likely be many legal conflicts among his staff. Mautner decided to call the California Attorney General's Office and ask if it would take over prosecution of the case. For some reason, that office declined to take over the case but instead agreed to furnish an investigator from the attorney general's office to assist with the Napa prosecution. At that point, Mautner began studying the Napa Police Department documents and reports in detail.

Mautner organized his evidence, and on Friday, December 22, 1989, he filed a criminal complaint against Hanson and Pitner. Hanson was arrested near his Napa residence that evening, and bail was initially set at $1 million. The police continued to search for Pitner. Hanson was charged with 320 criminal counts, including securities fraud, grand theft and burglary. The complaint also charged Pitner with 54 counts of similar violations.

On Tuesday, December 26, 1989, Pitner was arrested at his Sacramento residence by investigators from the district attorney's office. Pitner's bail was set at $500,000.

That same afternoon, David Hanson and Robert Pitner appeared in Napa Municipal Court on the charges of defrauding hundreds of investors in LendVest Mortgage company and Joseph Mathews Winery. Both Hanson and Pitner wore shackles into court. The courtroom was filled with many alleged victims in the case, people who had invested in the now-bankrupt companies and faced the possibility of losing most or all their money.

Municipal Court commissioner Marc Vieira presided over the proceedings. Michael Fallon, David Hanson's personal bankruptcy attorney, made a special appearance for Hanson, and told the court Hanson was indigent and could not afford to hire his own criminal defense attorney. In fact, Fallon accused District Attorney Jerry Mautner of "grandstanding" and argued that Hanson should be released on his own recognizance without the need to post bail. Fallon said that the millions of dollars missing from both LendVest and Joseph Mathews Winery complex "had absolutely and unequivocally nothing to do with David Hanson. It has to do with the bankruptcy system." Fallon's remarks brought boos and hoots of derisive laughter from the gallery.

Commissioner Vieira appointed the Napa County Public Defender's Office as counsel for Pitner. Napa defense attorney Mervin Lernhart was appointed to represent Hanson. Vieira then ordered the defendants be held overnight in the Napa County Jail, pending a bail hearing scheduled for Wednesday, December 27, 1989.

Left: Napa County district attorney Jerome Mautner. *Courtesy of Richard Bennett.*

Middle: Napa County Department of Corrections booking photo of David G. Hanson following his arrest on Friday, December 22, 1989. *Courtesy of Napa County Sheriff's Department.*

Right: Attorney Michael Fallon represented David Hanson in Hanson's personal Chapter 7 bankruptcy case. *Courtesy of Michael Fallon.*

On Wednesday, December 27, 1989, Commissioner Vieira denied Hanson and Pitner's request to be released on their own recognizance, but he did reduce bail for the two men. Hanson's bail was lowered from $1,000,000 to $750,000, and Pitner's from $500,000 to $250,000. Vieira also discussed setting a date for the preliminary hearing, a proceeding held before a judge to determine if there is enough evidence to justify holding the defendant or defendants to answer for the alleged charges. However, the newly appointed attorneys requested time to prepare before setting a specific date.

The case was continued several times, and eventually bail for Hanson was further lowered to $250,000. Hanson's attorney filed a writ of habeas corpus requesting a hearing after another magistrate refused to lower the bail even further during an April 11 hearing.

On Friday, May 25, 1990, Hanson's defense attorney at the time, Victor Amstadter, argued before visiting judge Donald Fretz that Hanson's custody was illegal because the bail was unreasonably high and not related to the crimes charged. Additionally, Amstadter argued that Hanson was unable to pay that amount of bail now that he had filed for personal bankruptcy.

In denying Hanson's petition, Judge Fretz acknowledged that Hanson's lack of violent criminal behavior could be one argument for reducing

Judge Donald Fretz denied David Hanson's request to reduce his bail. *Courtesy of Ann Fretz-Scott.*

bail. However, Hanson did "very considerable economic injury to many people," Fretz stated.

Fretz continued, "If a bank robber pulled off a $7 million robbery, the court's attitude would be to lock the door and throw away the key. I admit the method is different, but it also gets to the seriousness of the offenses as charged. The loss to those who lost it is real. The bail is reasonable, and the petition is denied."

Fretz's ruling on bail effectively left Hanson in Napa County jail.

Eventually, after several continuances, the preliminary hearing was set for June 18, 1990. The hearing commenced on that date and would not end until Wednesday September 5, 1990. Mautner represented the district attorney's office; Mervin Lernhart represented David Hanson; and Barry Levy represented Robert Pitner.

Judge David Otis from Siskiyou County was brought to Napa County to hear the LendVest case because the local judges had disqualified themselves. Judges must disqualify themselves if they believe there is a substantial doubt as to their capacity to be impartial. In a case with so many victims in a small community such as Napa, it would not be unusual for the local judges to have a personal relationship with one or more of those victims or someone connected to LendVest.

In one of the longest preliminary examinations in Napa history at that time, Mautner presented sufficient evidence to show the judge that there was indeed enough evidence to hold Hanson and Pitner for trial. In fact, if there was any doubt before the preliminary hearing of wrongdoing on Hanson's part, there was little doubt after the hearing. Attorneys labeled the case as the largest securities fraud case in the history of Napa County.

Mautner and defense attorneys summoned as many as two hundred witnesses, including LendVest employees, ready to testify about the intricate system allegedly used to bilk hundreds of people out of their money, including some who lost their life savings.

The testimony was sometimes emotional. Witnesses described Hanson as confident and intimidating, using his position in what appeared to be a successful company and his respect in the community to woo new investors.

"He was the pillar of the community, the family man, a churchgoing man—trustworthy," said Marlene Dones, who had worked at LendVest as an insurance manager and invested $75,000 in the company. "A lot of elderly people were investing with him, including several ministers. I figured it would be a good deal."

Lured by the attractively high interest rates and the perception that LendVest was a prosperous and growing company, investors by the hundreds poured money into the mortgage company.

Concurrently with their investments, witnesses testified, the company was drawing up two sets of financial papers so LendVest could continue to provide federal Department of Housing and Urban Development loans and maintain a line of credit with local banks. Witnesses alleged one set of financial statements showed a prospering company, while the other showed LendVest slipping quickly into massive debt. Of course, the legitimate financial statement showing LendVest was a failing organization was purposefully not shown to the investors.

In front of a packed courtroom crowded with observers—including many LendVest victims and employees—Judge Otis held that Robert Pitner would be held for trial on only fifteen of the thirty-four counts charged against him, which included embezzlement and securities fraud.

Judge Otis had harsh words for Hanson, who slumped in his chair. "Mr. Hanson, at the time you first addressed this court you said that you should be dressed in business attire because you are a businessman. I think that even though you may have been a businessman with respect to these charges, that you are guilty of fraud and deceit and through your actions you have caused the ruin of a great number of people in this community." Then, Judge Otis ruled that Hanson must stand trial and immediately doubled Hanson's bail to $500,000.

Investors who packed the Hall of Justice courtroom reacted to the decision with both relief and trepidation, knowing that they would have to testify again when the case went to trial. After the order was announced, Tony Aniello pumped his fist in the air. He had lost $120,000 when LendVest went bankrupt. "That's the best thing I have heard since I was born," an excited Aniello said. "I'm glad the judge threw the book at him."

Now that Hanson and Pitner had been held to answer by the judge, Mautner prepared a document that accurately conformed to the preliminary judge's rulings. The result was a document called the "Information," which contained the formal criminal charges the defendants would face at their respective jury trials.

Victims varied in age, gender and financial expertise, and Mautner wanted to ensure that Hanson was charged with every crime he had committed. Charges of 139 counts of fraud, embezzlement and burglary against David Hanson were filed in Napa Superior Court on September 18, 1990.

1. Eighty counts of violating Corporations Code Section 25401, which makes it a crime to sell a security in California by making any fraudulent statements or omissions.

2. Two counts of violating Business and Professions Code Section 10238.6, which makes it a crime to submit false financial statements to the Department of Real Estate when applying for a real property securities permit.

3. Thirty-seven violations of Corporations Code Section 25110, which stipulates that it is a crime in California to sell an unqualified security. (A security sale is qualified by applying for approval of the Department of Corporations.)

4. Thirteen counts of Penal Code Section 487 violations—in other words, grand theft. Grand theft, in 1991, was defined as stealing money or property worth more than $400 in money or other items of value, such as trust deeds. Grand theft charges involved Hanson's theft of money or trust deeds from both investors and his own company.

5. Seven counts of Penal Code Section 459 violations—in essence, residential burglary. Residential burglary is defined as entering a residence in order to commit theft or any felony.

In this case, Mautner charged the sale or attempted sale of an unqualified security as the felony that would qualify the crime as a felony burglary. Mautner explained his thinking as follows: the sale or attempted sale of a security by *any* fraudulent means is a felony. In some of the crimes charged, Hanson had entered some potential investors' residences to sell unqualified securities and had used fraudulent means in doing so. Each time he did this, he was committing a felony residential burglary. Residential burglary carried more prison time than any of the other charges in the case. Thanks to his scholarly approach to the law, Mautner spotted the elements of residential burglary as a crime in this case, and he charged every count he believed legally applied.

Sentence enhancements applied to one hundred of the counts, due to the extraordinary amount of money involved. Enhancements increased the maximum possible prison time.

In pretrial hearings, Hanson and Pitner each entered pleas of not guilty and were granted separate trials. Their attorneys also filed motions for change of venue due to the concern that the defendants could not get a fair trial locally. Indeed, Napa contained a host of alleged victims, and there had been much publicity in the local media about the financial devastation experienced by many of the town's citizens. The judge agreed with Hanson and Pitner's attorneys and granted each of them their motions to change venue. As a result, Hanson's case would be tried in Yolo County. Pitner's case would be tried in Lake County. Ultimately, the charges against Pitner were dismissed by the Lake County district attorney.

Napa County district attorney Jerome Mautner was up for reelection in November 1990, and his deputy, Anthony Perez, was his opponent. During the campaign, Mautner assigned Perez as the trial deputy for the LendVest case, and this particular assignment caused some stir in the district attorney's office.

There was some speculation that Mautner had assigned the case to Perez as payback for his running against Mautner. It was also probable that most deputy district attorneys would not want the case because of its complexity with hundreds of victims and hundreds of exhibits encompassing thousands of document pages, which would require a massive effort to organize. Further, Perez was a relatively inexperienced attorney. In his private practice, he had been an associate attorney assisting the lead trial attorney in the only

Left: All fraud charges against Robert Pitner were ultimately dismissed. *Courtesy of Napa County Historical Society.*

Right: Anthony Perez. *Courtesy of the Napa County District Attorney's Office.*

serious felony case on his résumé, and he was far from being a lead attorney in the district attorney's office.

Some observers suspected Mautner selected Perez as a setup, hoping he would botch the case. However, Mautner truly wanted justice, and he would not purposely jeopardize a trial involving so many victims by assigning the case to an attorney who was not qualified to handle it. Perhaps Mautner's rationale in assigning the case to Perez was that if Perez did win the election, he could assign the case to whomever he deemed appropriate. And that is exactly what happened: Perez defeated Mautner and would take office as the Napa County district attorney in January 1991.

10

THE PROSECUTION'S CASE AGAINST DAVID HANSON

Perez began working on the case with his assigned investigator, Ed Wynn. The defense attorney was Mervin Lernhart, generally regarded as Napa County's premier criminal defense attorney. He was a highly skilled trial attorney who had been practicing law since the late 1960s and was more experienced than any other defense attorney in Napa.

Anthony Perez was now responsible for all case assignments, having defeated Jerome Mautner in the election and taken over as Napa County district attorney on January 7, 1991. Mautner was now gone, and all office decisions were up to Perez. Almost immediately, he assigned the LendVest case to deputy district attorney Stephen Kroyer. Kroyer later recalled Perez telling him, "You are the best trial lawyer in the office, and the case is important to the district attorney's office and the citizens of Napa County."

Stephen T. Kroyer was born in Fort Riley, Kansas, and graduated from Rice University in 1972 with a degree in political science. In 1974, a close family relative was the victim of a violent crime, and this tragedy motivated Kroyer to enroll at Western State University College of Law. After graduation, he was hired by the Napa County District Attorney's Office. Here, he gained years of trial experience, becoming one of the top trial attorneys in Napa. He rarely lost a case. Now, he was taking on the LendVest case, and preparation was a complicated process.

Kroyer was eager to take on the challenge. However, even a trial lawyer of Kroyer's ability was facing difficult circumstances. First, the date had already been set for trial, and it was coming up in about three weeks. Second, this case had multiple victims and copious documents to assess.

Left: Mervin Lernhart was David Hanson's attorney. *Courtesy of Barbara Lernhart.*

Middle: Deputy District Attorney Steven T. Kroyer prosecuted the case against David Hanson. He later became a Napa County Superior Court judge. He is now retired. *Courtesy of Steven T. Kroyer.*

Right: Napa County district attorney investigator Ed Wynn. *Courtesy of Ed Wynn.*

Investigator Ed Wynn was also well qualified and experienced. He was a former Marine and highly decorated Vietnam veteran with a long career in law enforcement. Kroyer knew he was fortunate to have Wynn as his investigator.

Wynn had already put in many hours on the case, organizing the voluminous documents, and he was elated to be working with Kroyer, knowing that he would organize the case better for trial than most. Thanks to Wynn's efforts, in a short period of time, Kroyer was able to get up to speed on this complex case.

To try this case, Kroyer and investigator Ed Wynn had to give up their current caseloads to devote all their time to preparing for the trial, which involved visiting the victims, listening to their stories and observing how personally devastated they were. "These stories were gut-wrenching," Wynn recalled. "We had victims approaching their eighties; some of these elderly people had to go back to work for the rest of their lives."

One victim who especially touched Wynn was an elderly man who had large amounts of money in several banks. The man was an alcoholic, and David Hanson knew this. When this gentleman was clearly under the influence, Hanson took him to each of his banks to withdraw substantial sums of money for Hanson to "invest." Many of the victims were elderly. One law enforcement officer who had lost his savings and retirement fund had also convinced friends to invest in deals that Hanson was promoting.

This man was so emotionally upset that Wynn feared he would suffer health problems or might even attempt to harm Hanson.

Preparing for the trial, Kroyer and Wynn stayed in a Woodland hotel and spent each evening preparing for the next day's witnesses, which was a complicated process. The defense team, consisting of attorney Mervin Lernhart; his investigator, Patrick McGreal; and Lernhart's spouse and administrative assistant, Barbara Lernhart, also set up shop in Woodland, renting an apartment and devoting one entire room to analyzing investigation reports and making trial preparations.

THE TRIAL BEGINS

Opening statements commenced on Monday, August 5, 1991, in Woodland, California, before a Yolo County jury with Yolo County Superior Court judge Stephen Mock presiding. Prosecuting attorney Stephen Kroyer strode to face the jury and wasted no time in painting a picture of David Hanson, the former LendVest president, as a conniving cheater who lived high on the hog with his investors' hard-earned money and, when he knew his schemes were unraveling, lied to potential investors to solicit even more funds.

"Many people trusted Hanson; in some cases, they entrusted him with their life savings," Kroyer stated. "In the end, they were left holding pieces of paper worth nothing."

Defense attorney Mervin Lernhart described David Hanson as a man who had helped countless Napa residents financially over the years but, after the failure of a legitimate business venture, fell victim to community wrath. "There is understandable bitterness in a small town when a significant number of people lose their savings," he said, suggesting this might have been the impetus behind the criminal charges against his client.

Despite the complexity of the case, Lernhart continued, jurors would have to decide "whether the issue is about a group of people who lost money on a business venture, or whether David

Judge Stephen Mock. *Courtesy of Lisa Fitt.*

99

Hanson—who has spent much of his life in the town of Napa—really intended to rip people off. Now Mr. Hanson stands accused of 139 criminal counts. The man everyone came to when they needed a home loan is now the villain." The defense attorney concluded by saying, "You must decide whether that is true."

Prosecuting attorney Kroyer had the burden of proving the truth of the charges against Hanson beyond a reasonable doubt. In his opening statement, he had summarized what had happened at LendVest and how it had fooled investors. Now he would prove his case by calling the following witnesses.

NAPA CERTIFIED PUBLIC ACCOUNTANT ERIC LEHMAN

Eric Lehman had been working with bankruptcy trustee Charles Sims reviewing documents recovered from LendVest, and he was able to reconstruct LendVest's accounting system between 1984 and 1988, which was the focus of the criminal case. Lehman testified that Hanson had maintained two very different financial statements showing vastly different figures describing the financial health of the company. One financial record, used for tax purposes and to secure lines of credit, showed a dynamic, financially stable company. The other financial record clearly demonstrated that LendVest was losing vast sums of money.

Lehman's reconstruction of financial records involved tracing every canceled check to see who had cashed it and where the money had gone. Lehman testified, "LendVest about broke even" from 1981 to 1983, but one year later the system of double financial statements began. That year, the company "lost a substantial amount of money and could be described as insolvent." Every year after that, Lehman testified, "The company lost increasing amounts of money. By 1988, about two hundred individuals held payable LendVest promissory notes totaling more than $7.9 million. But at the same time, net income was approaching a $3 million loss."

Lehman also noted that records indicated Hanson was transferring large sums of money to the Joseph Mathews Winery and to another subsidiary that was also losing money. When asked how Hanson had paid his bills, Lehman testified that during the last three months before LendVest went out of business, Hanson borrowed money from individual investors at the rate of $300,000 per month.

LENDVEST EMPLOYEE MARY PORT

Mary Port, a LendVest official, testified that on two separate occasions Hanson ordered her to alter LendVest's tax returns to show that the business was financially healthy. With his questions, Kroyer connected Port's testimony with that of Eric Lehman about altering tax returns and Lehman's finding one tax return with Wite-Out correction fluid applied all over it.

Port also described other illegalities for which Hanson was responsible, including (1) having other employees alter their required financial statements to show they were in less debt than they really were. According to her, when some employees balked, Hanson simply said, "Do it," in a flat voice; (2) receiving double profit by assigning the same trust deed for a $49,000 loan to two different people when there should be only one deed holder; and (3) signing false employment verification forms for nonexistent workers.

Port also testified that Hanson maintained a lavish lifestyle that included a Porsche company car, his own Mercedes and a lovely home. She described extravagant company-funded parties, including a 1987 Christmas party held at the Joseph Mathews Winery only six months before LendVest ceased doing business.

CERTIFIED PUBLIC ACCOUNTANT HARVEY GRANT

Harvey Grant's testimony was straightforward, focusing on the false financial statements and tax returns he had prepared. With each financial document Kroyer showed to Grant, the witness was asked if he had prepared it. "Yes," Grant stated.

Kroyer then asked if the document was false. Again, Grant answered, "Yes."

Grant acknowledged that his conduct in preparing false financial statements and false tax returns was criminal, but he indicated he had made a deal with the prosecution. He would testify truthfully against Hanson and plead guilty to both of his offenses, and his sentence would be eight months in jail and a fine.

WITNESSES REPRESENTING FINANCIAL INSTITUTIONS

Witnesses from the Department of Real Estate, Bank of America and the Department of Veteran's Affairs testified that in 1986, 1987 and 1988, Hanson had failed to submit documents that accurately reflected LendVest's financial condition. Had these organizations known of LendVest's precarious financial status, the Department of Real Estate would not have issued real property security permits; the VA would not have allowed LendVest to participate in its loan program; and Bank of America would have refused to extend credit.

FORMER LENDVEST EMPLOYEE MARTINA HARTUNG

Martina Hartung testified that in 1981, she was hired as a receptionist at LendVest and subsequently worked her way up into more responsible positions. In 1987, she was flattered when David Hanson offered to let her purchase 2 percent of the company's stock. Hanson told her the company was doing well, and he wanted to let some employees have a say in its direction. He also offered her a promotion and a substantial salary increase. Hanson did not indicate that the company had debts as well as a negative worth.

When Hartung told Hanson she wanted to talk his offer over with her husband, he stated that she did not have a lot of time and pointedly reminded her that other employees had lost the chance to invest by making a similar request. "He said if you didn't trust and believe in him, he didn't want you on his team," she testified. She and her husband ended up investing $75,000, as well as $15,000 of her grandmother's money. They lost it all.

Hartung also testified that she brought in a friend, David James, who testified that in December 1987 he had invested $75,000 and was to receive a trust deed to some Marin County property. However, the deed was never recorded in his name, and one day after James's investment, the deed was assigned to a thrift (savings and loan) company.

DOROTHY PARKER

Dorothy Parker described how her mother, a Napa resident, suggested that she invest $125,000 from the 1987 sale of her San Jose house with LendVest. "I thought it sounded good," said Parker, sixty-five, who then met with Hanson in her mother's home and wrote the check. However, Parker testified, except for receiving her monthly interest payments, that was the last she ever saw of her investment. "If it weren't for my children, I would be a bag lady."

Mae Dugan

Octogenarian Mae Dugan testified that a friend had referred her to Hanson, who belonged to her church. "He said LendVest was the fastest-growing mortgage company in the state and was sound as a dollar." She further stated that Hanson "was immaculately dressed" and had Christian employees who conducted business "in a Christian manner."

After several visits to her home, Hanson persuaded her to take out a trust deed on the home of another family she knew. He pledged his assets to secure the loan, which made her feel secure. "The monthly interest was always paid, and I trusted him completely for future investments." She lost her total investment of $65,000.

Ardis Jabs

Ardis Jabs, eighty-four, had met Hanson at church. She testified that she first invested $191,000 in LendVest in exchange for an interest-only note, and she never asked him for details on where the money was going because "I trusted him. He was a friend, and I thought how fortunate I was to have someone take care of me, take care of my business."

Jabs made subsequent investments with LendVest. She said she became a member of LendVest Mortgage Fund II at Hanson's suggestion, and she let him fill out all the forms, which included a power of attorney. She said she did not understand what power of attorney meant and at the time did not realize that it gave Hanson legal authority to sign documents for her without her knowing about it.

Jabs's total losses amounted to $256,000.

Bea Odle

Bea Odle, seventy-six, began investing with Hanson several years after meeting him in church. She and her husband, Lou—also seventy-six—

started with $80,000 after Hanson assured her that "our pastor had invested with him." Hanson said he "was taking care of the pastor and could do well for us." Ultimately, the Odles invested $160,000. Except for receiving timely interest payments on their investment, they lost the entire $160,000.

RON WALKER

Walker was a young man in his forties who testified that from 1983 until LendVest's closing in 1988, he had invested a total of $340,000. He said that Hanson assured him his investment would be secured with real property, and he pointed out that Walker always received his interest checks on time. When his original $290,000 investment came due, Hanson persuaded him to increase his stake and change it into a general corporate trust account that was being pooled to invest in commercial property. Hanson showed him financial documents, and Walker stated that "the company looked very profitable to me."

Ron Walker was defrauded out of $340,000 by David Hanson. *Courtesy of Ron Walker.*

Walker was devastated by his $340,000 loss.

JENNIFER JORDAN

Jennifer Jordan, a single mother in her thirties, testified about her failed efforts to retrieve a $38,000 investment from Hanson. She later discovered that her investment was not secured, as Hanson had promised. "I don't have to worry because my investment is secured, right?" she asked him, and he responded, "Maybe not." Jordan stated she could not understand how her investment was not secured. Later, through her own investigation, she discovered that although she had received documents from LendVest saying she was part of a trust deed, her name had never been added to the deed that was the security for her investment. She lost all her money.

GARDNER LEIGHTON

Hanson's sale of an unsecured note in May 1988 to Gardner Leighton constituted another criminal count against him. Leighton had met Hanson at the health club to which they both belonged. After Leighton refinanced his home through LendVest, Hanson convinced him to invest a portion of the refinancing proceeds, telling him that LendVest was solid and in good financial condition. Hanson even showed him a company balance sheet reflecting a healthy financial status.

Leighton indicated that he wanted to invest in secured notes, such as second deeds of trust, and purchased one trust deed from Hanson for $51,000 and a second trust deed for $21,000. Leighton also signed a power of attorney document in Hanson's favor on both investments after Hanson assured him it could not be used to sell or transfer the investments. "They would not be used for anything other than servicing." However, Hanson used the powers of attorney to convey both trust deeds to third parties, substituting unsecured promissory notes for Leighton's deeds of trust. Leighton and his wife lost their entire investment.

LEAH HAND

Leah Hand lost $140,000. She testified that Hanson gave her a note secured by a deed of trust, stating that LendVest would take over the loan if the property owner ever defaulted. However, she testified, she never received the actual deed of trust, and Hanson did not tell her he had assigned the same security she had purchased to a savings and loan company.

THOMAS REDMON

Thomas Redmon testified that he was given a promissory note for his initial $30,000 investment and thought he would be receiving a deed of trust. Instead, LendVest officers recorded the deed of trust to a financial institution. "I thought it was mine, my security," Redmon testified. He lost a total of $69,000.

HAROLD TURNER

Another criminal count was based on Hanson's sale of an unsecured promissory note to Harold Turner. In 1983, Turner held a real estate license. He testified that he had prior investment experience in real estate and certificates of deposit and said that Hanson assured him of the company's stability. Turner had previously invested in a company that had declared bankruptcy, so he requested financial information. Hanson showed him LendVest financial statements reflecting a positive net worth. Still reluctant to invest, Turner requested even more information, whereupon Hanson pointed to a stack of envelopes and said they were FHA and VA loan applications and intimated that LendVest held a unique position with the VA and the FHA. He also alluded to his $25,000-per-month salary.

Turner subsequently invested $115,000 in LendVest, stating that he was relying on Hanson's continual assurances of the company's financial health. Turner also said he was receiving his monthly interest payments. Ultimately, the interest payments ceased, and Turner lost his investment.

WILLIAM BARTLETT

William Bartlett was a neighbor of the minister of Hanson's church, who spoke highly of Hanson and vouched for his honesty. The minister also said he himself had made a large investment in LendVest.

Hanson told Bartlett he was one of the three top people in the state who could provide VA and FHA loans. Bartlett testified that "he figured that it was a pretty good investment and invested $100,000 in trust deeds." But although Hanson promised to deliver these deeds of trust connected to his investments, Bartlett never received them. He lost his entire $100,000 investment.

JAMES ROGERS

James Rogers purchased a promissory note in June 1987 after Rogers's wife met Hanson at the First Baptist Church in Napa where they both served on the church board. Hanson convinced Rogers's wife to take out a $50,000 VA loan on her house, and he then persuaded her to invest the $50,000 in an unsecured interest-only note. After Mrs. Rogers sold her home, Hanson convinced her and her husband to combine the $25,000 from the sale and the previous $50,000 into a new note for $75,000. According to Rogers, "Hanson characterized himself as a man of integrity and honesty and promised he would handle the money honestly." He did not. James Rogers and his wife lost their entire investments.

JOHN SIDORSKI

John Sidorski. *Courtesy of John Sidorski.*

In March 1988, Hanson sold a promissory note to local high school teacher John Sidorski. Sidorski said he "knew that Hanson was a religious, God-fearing man and that he was on the Christian School Board." His initial investment was $50,000, invested in the Joseph Mathews Winery. Based on financial projections made by CPA Harvey Grant, which showed the winery to be profitable, Sidorski invested an additional $50,000 and also purchased from LendVest an interest-only promissory note in the amount of $20,628. Hanson assured Sidorski the winery was doing well. It was not. Sidorski lost over $120,000.

CHARLES THOMAS

Seventy-five-year-old Charles Thomas was a retired pool table salesman. He became one of the original limited partners in the Joseph Mathews Winery, and in making his investment, he relied on a prospectus describing the winery's projected profits. Thomas testified that Hanson personally guaranteed the investment and "that was the clincher." He admitted that he was an unsophisticated investor and did not read all the documents involved, but altogether, he invested approximately $200,000 in Hanson's companies.

Having lost his investment, Thomas was forced to go back to work. "I thought I would be retired by this time, but now I am selling pool tables again."

Edmund Hand

In April 1987, Hanson sold Edmund Hand an interest-only, unsecured promissory note amounting to $40,000 with LendVest. That $40,000 came from two notes Hand had previously invested with Hanson. Hand testified that he had "relied on Hanson's skill, expertise and honesty" and added that Hanson had told him nothing negative about his companies. Hand lost his total investment.

William Partain

William Partain was the former Napa County Airport director. He testified that Hanson told him he had moved Partain's entire $103,000 investment into a LendVest II account, even though Partain had never requested this, nor had Hanson ever discussed this transfer with him.

Partain said Hanson portrayed LendVest II as "sort of an elite-type situation" which they would be joining with investors who were doctors and lawyers. However, Hanson neglected to tell him and his wife that it was a long-term commitment of funds.

"I'm going to be seventy on my next birthday," he said. "I don't need that kind of investment." Then, when he read the booklet about LendVest II that Hanson sent to him, he discovered he could not retrieve his money without agreement of the general partnership, and not until much later did Partain see the fine print naming Hanson and two other LendVest executives as the fund's limited partners "who would receive substantial compensation through loans to be serviced by LendVest." Hanson transferred Partain's funds into the LendVest II account just three months before the company went bankrupt.

Donald Rooney

Donald Rooney, age sixty-nine, testified that in February 1988, he transferred $20,000 from his Individual Retirement Account (IRA) to LendVest. Rooney said he thought it was a secure account, but "I never received the deed of trust." Unfortunately, things got worse fast. One month later, Hanson convinced him to refinance his house, which was nearly paid off, and he put the $131,500 amount in LendVest's unsecured fund, from which he would receive interest that would cover his new house payments.

"I said I never did want to tie up my house," Rooney testified. "My goal in life was paying it off." Hanson had persuaded him by promising to back Rooney with his own interest in the Joseph Mathews Winery. Instead, both LendVest and the winery failed and went into bankruptcy. That left Rooney with a monthly house payment of $1,300 and a new mortgage that extended for another thirty years. Prior to refinancing his home, Rooney's mortgage payment was $169 per month and only months away from being paid off.

KATHY HUEY

Kathy Huey testified that she had been Hanson's employee since 1982 and was the only LendVest employee to decline David Hanson's offer to purchase stock in the company. She said she thought the stock purchase offer sounded good, but after discussing it with her husband, they decided to pass. "It just wasn't the right time for us," she recalled. "Hanson was upset with me and said, 'You will never be any more than a peon in the company. Only the owners will have advancement; you're making a very big mistake.'"

After this conversation, she continued to work for Hanson but said she felt "Dave looked at me a little differently." Other employees who did buy stock in the company testified that after Huey declined to buy stock, Hanson ostracized her. In 1987, she and her husband agreed to invest $50,000 in the Joseph Mathews Winery. The Hueys lost their entire investment.

The damage done to Napa citizens was powerful and damning evidence against Hanson. Many of the witnesses were elderly. Some were emotional, while others were calm as they testified about their personal experiences. It was clear, however, that they each had suffered substantial losses by investing in LendVest and believing Hanson's false representations.

Prosecuting attorney Stephen Kroyer then decided not to call any additional witnesses. He had calculated the maximum sentence he could get with the witnesses who had already testified, and he rested his case to save time for the jury and further hardship on witnesses who had not yet testified.

Now it was time for the defense to present its case.

11

THE DEFENSE OF DAVID HANSON

Defense attorney Mervin Lernhart opened the defense by calling David Hanson's corporate and personal attorney, Don Logan, to testify. Lernhart's questions concerned the legal setups behind both the LendVest companies and the Joseph Mathews Winery to show that (1) Hanson's transactions with investors were part of a normal course of business and (2) that investors had sufficient information on which to make investment decisions.

ATTORNEY DON LOGAN TESTIFIES

Logan described at length the mechanics of stock transfers by which Hanson gradually spread ownership of the company to several employees, as occurs in many growing businesses. He testified that he had prepared the paperwork for the 1987 recapitalization of the Joseph Mathews Winery, in which Hanson had an indirect involvement via LendVest and an entity called D&S Hanson Enterprises.

Pursuant to Hanson's requests, Logan prepared forms disclosing pertinent details to current and prospective shareholders. He stated that he wanted investors acquiring stock to know LendVest had loaned $1.3 million to the winery. "Investors were advised they would eventually be converted from creditors to limited partners, but at a decreased value," and that Hanson "had a substantial ownership interest in both entities."

Don Logan was David Hanson's corporate and personal attorney. *Courtesy of Napa County Historical Society.*

Logan further testified, "This put shareholders on notice about what I felt was a conflict of interest." He also stated that the prospectus he prepared advised potential investors of a $400,000 debt to another Hanson-controlled company, Napa Valley Distributing, and a $50,000 unsecured debt to its owner.

He went on to say he had no idea that LendVest was in serious financial trouble at the time or that it was regularly helping to meet the winery payroll. "The prospectus stated that his law firm was not representing LendVest or the winery in this matter and urged potential investors to consult their own attorneys for advice."

On Kroyer's cross-examination, Logan admitted that in March or April 1988, Hanson repaid a $20,000 loan from him. This was at the same time many other investors were unsuccessfully requesting return of their money and shortly before Hanson's company went into bankruptcy. On further cross-examination, Kroyer elicited testimony that Hanson had told Logan he had removed investors' names from trust deeds without their consent. It was Kroyer's hope that his cross-examination of Logan would diminish Logan's credibility in front of the jury, as his testimony showed that he was able to fully recoup his investment when other investors could not.

LENDVEST EXECUTIVE DON LEMMONS

Lernhart then called LendVest executive Don Lemmons to the witness stand. Lemmons had known Hanson since 1976, when the two of them worked for a Vallejo mortgage company. When Hanson branched out on his own in Napa, Lemmons followed him and in 1981 became a 5 percent stockholder in LendVest. He became a corporate officer and director in the company and in the early 1980s moved from working on commission to a small salary plus commission. With the company's expansion in the middle of the decade, the Vallejo office alone brought in about $90,000 per month plus commissions, for a total monthly income of about $150,000 in 1986, and Lemmons then commanded a larger salary.

Lemmons testified he "had all the faith in the world in the business" and that Hanson would "pull us out of the situation" by opening a Sacramento office in early 1988.

Lemmons further stated that he also invested in the Joseph Mathews Winery project, which he considered a good long-term investment, although during his testimony his recollection of the actual amounts varied. He had "borrowed about $500,000 from LendVest to pay off other debts, but that this was not unusual for a 'family organization' that tried to help its employees."

Don Lemmons was a former LendVest executive. *Courtesy of Lisa Fitt.*

In a blistering cross-examination, Lemmons admitted that Hanson told him he had falsified company financial documents to show a positive net worth.

Lemmons's further testimony revealed that he "did not care" about Hanson's falsifying company financial documents to show a positive net worth. He believed in Hanson and felt he would pull them out of the difficulty.

Kroyer then asked Lemmons what he thought of Hanson now. "He's a good friend," Lemmons responded. "I support him all the way."

During a frequently acerbic cross-examination, Lemmons pointed out that none of the banks or agencies had filed any charges against LendVest on the basis of any losses. When pressed, however, he acknowledged that he ceased working at LendVest in 1988 and had no firsthand knowledge of the company after it declared bankruptcy.

Lemmons also admitted that senior LendVest employees often delayed cashing their paychecks because they knew the company periodically had insufficient funds, even though Hanson told investors their money was secure.

"This was happening when you couldn't even cash your own payroll?" Kroyer asked.

"Yes," Lemmons replied. "It had to do with our potential. I had all the faith in the world in what we were doing." Lemmons further testified that he did not know Hanson had a personal financial stake in Napa Valley Distributing, a company that also received LendVest loans, but he stated he saw nothing wrong with it, as long as Hanson had other assets and "could deal with it" if the distributing company lost money.

Under further cross-examination, Lemmons testified that he did not know LendVest was making the Joseph Mathews Winery payroll at the time of its 1987 restructuring, but he said the winery "probably would have found financing elsewhere" had LendVest money been unavailable.

Kroyer then pointed out several other discrepancies between the company's tax returns and Lemmons' memory of his salary; Lemmons admitted his memory could have been faulty.

Kroyer then asked, "Can you think of any other answers you gave on direct examination that you could also be off on?"

His cross-examination became so heated that investigator Ed Wynn recalled Lemmons becoming flustered on the witness stand and blurting, "Mr. Kroyer, what do you want me to say?" Kroyer responded that all he wanted was the truth.

FORMER LENDVEST OFFICIAL DAVID DICKSON

David Dickson was a former LendVest official, and his testimony reinforced the concept of a healthy, growing company that took good care of its employees and ran into trouble only after the IRS investigation stemming from the May 1988 Drug Tug bust in San Francisco Bay, in which the IRS seized narcotics and money, of which $104,000 was owned by LendVest. The newspapers reported that money invested seven months earlier in LendVest was profit from an earlier drug run. After no connection was found, this money was eventually returned to LendVest, but the damage was done. An investor run on LendVest had started.

David Dickson further testified that after the Drug Tug incident and the subsequent IRS investigation, crucial lines of bank credit dried up and prevented LendVest from conducting business. Dickson also blamed media attention. "The press publicity had a negative impact on people with outstanding loans, who then called in and demanded their money. All we could do was take their request and have somebody decide what to do with it."

Lernhart then asked, "Was that when LendVest went belly-up?"

Dickson responded, "Yes."

Under Kroyer's cross-examination, Dickson said he thought he was on the company's board of directors, but he was not sure. He testified that Hanson told him he was on the board, but he had not been invited to attend any meetings. Dickson also admitted that Hanson had approached him on the three investments he had made in the Joseph Mathews Winery, although Hanson had not mentioned that a San Jose accounting firm had recommended that the winery declare bankruptcy. Dickson also testified that Hanson had not consulted him when he loaned company money to the winery or to the Napa Valley Distributing Company, in which Hanson held majority ownership.

Hanson did not ask permission when he borrowed LendVest money himself, nor had Dickson tracked how much Hanson paid back. "I was just doing my job," he testified, "and I thought other people were just doing theirs."

LendVest Employee Jeff Moore

Jeff Moore took over LendVest shortly after the IRS investigation and Hanson's subsequent removal as president. He testified that more than $100,000 seized by the IRS was needed for daily company operations, and that loss hurt the business even more than losing bank lines of credit. "We couldn't make the following week's payroll and effectively had to lay off the entire company. The company could have survived by reverting to its beginnings as a mortgage brokerage firm, but its financial difficulties were compounded by spooked investor demands for repayment in the wake of publicity about the IRS investigation."

Moore acknowledged that LendVest's capital had been stretched thin by opening the Sacramento office and by a downturn in the economy, but the volume of investments the new office was expected to garner made him confident about the company's prospects.

In a rare light moment in the trial, especially during cross-examination, Moore acknowledged there were no other candidates to head the company at the point when he took over. "It was kind of like being handed a bucket after the *Titanic* hit the iceberg."

Moore went on to testify that he still considered Hanson a friend, but he was unaware that Hanson had removed investors' names from trust deeds. Moore said he was filing for bankruptcy.

Outside of the jury's presence, the trial judge, Stephen Mock, ruled that should Hanson take the witness stand, he would permit the prosecution to bring up Hanson's 1990 federal conviction for currency structuring.

Therefore, to avoid the jury's hearing about this prior conviction, Lernhart advised Hanson not to testify. However, in lieu of Hanson's testimony, Lernhart called Hanson's wife, Sandra.

Sandra Hanson, David Hanson's Wife

In a soft, clear voice, Sandra Hanson testified that her husband did not enter people's homes intending to take their money (the basis of the prosecutor's burglary charges). Instead, she testified that a visit to the Hawaiian home of part-time Napa resident Harold Langdon had only social motivations. "No papers were signed, and no money was exchanged during the visit." However, Langdon received a Joseph Mathews Winery prospectus and had questioned Hanson about it. Previous witnesses had established that Hanson was part owner of the winery and that LendVest lent substantial operating capital to the winery to keep it afloat.

Similarly, in a visit by Hanson to the home of William Partain, the former Napa Airport director then living in Vacaville, no business was discussed "until at least after lunch. Mr. Partain indicated he would consider investing in LendVest Mortgage Fund II, although no papers were signed, and no money changed hands."

Under cross-examination, Kroyer attacked Sandra Hanson's credibility, asking if she was still friends with former LendVest officials Don Lemmons, Dave Dickson, Mary Port and Jeff Moore, all of whom had testified in the trial.

When Kroyer asked if she ever discussed the case or her upcoming testimony with either her husband, his defense attorney or the defense investigator, Hanson grew audibly agitated. Her voice rose in pitch, and she spoke faster, sounding nervous and angry. At first, she denied any such conversations, but when pressed, she reversed her previous testimony and admitted that she had discussed parts of her expected testimony with her husband. "Mr. Hanson did ask me about the topics to be covered in the trial, and I told him what I remembered."

Kroyer then asked again about the Hawaii visit. She testified that the visit was very pleasant and had only social motivations. She was with her husband the entire time and did not see Harold Langdon give her husband a $600 check. This contradicted both Langdon's testimony and the photocopy of a canceled check.

Kroyer now revisited the William Partain matter. By now, Sandra Hanson's voice had grown louder and stronger. She testified that her husband never said he had put Partain's money into LendVest II before the visit to his home or asked Partain if he concurred with the prospect.

Her understanding was that "Partain's money from his IRA account went directly into LendVest II only a few months before the original LendVest company went into bankruptcy." This contradicted Partain's testimony that Hanson told him he had transferred Partain's entire $103,000 investment into LendVest II without first seeking his permission.

Following Sandra Hanson's testimony, Lernhart indicated that the defense would rest; it had presented all the witnesses and had no other evidence to offer.

12

CLOSING ARGUMENTS

Prosecuting attorney Stephen Kroyer began by thanking the jury members for serving on the seven-week trial. "The American system of justice could not survive without jurors such as you, and I know it can be a burdensome and thankless job for each of you." He then announced to them that Hanson was "one of the most impressive, smooth-talking liars and cheaters you'll ever come across. He looks like a nice man and goes to great lengths to make the community think he is a good Christian and a prosperous businessman. But this is just a front. Hanson may have had some legitimate business activities, but that was only to hide his other, illegal activities."

Kroyer went on: "Some of the investors had no idea what was happening to them until it was too late, and Hanson wreaked havoc in the lives of many people. He couldn't make it as a legitimate businessman, and the right thing for him to have done would be to accept that and move on. Instead, he took his investors' money.

"By the end of the 1983–1984 fiscal year," Kroyer continued, "accountant Harvey Grant felt compelled to include his written concerns on the company's annual financial statement. Hanson did not do the right thing. Instead, he caused false financial statements to be created every single month from 1984 to 1988 to make LendVest look like a financially healthy company so he could persuade people to invest in it. But instead of investing their money in anything legitimate, he kept most of it for himself. He used what investors gave him to pay the interest to the first-generation of investors, then second-generation investors, and then third-generation investors until he got in over his head and no longer had enough money coming in to pay the interest on all these investments.

"LendVest continued with lines of credit and the ability to sell securities by falsifying documents submitted to banks and government agencies. Hanson used money he took from investors for his lavish lifestyle, which included expensive cars for himself and his family and a huge annual salary of $300,000. He also used investors' money, without their knowledge or consent, to prop up ancillary businesses in which he either had a large stake or which he controlled outright. These investments included the Napa Valley Distributing company, Joseph Mathews Winery and LendVest Mortgage Fund II.

"Hanson was running a 'shell game,' and what kept it going was his ability to go out and get more money. He lied to prospective investors about the company's health, despite the law that required him to tell the truth. Some of his employees knew that everything was not aboveboard, but Hanson was able to buy their silence by giving them huge salary increases—up to $110,000 in several cases, for instance with Don Lemmons and possibly Dickson. Also, he got another employee, Martina Hartung, originally a receptionist, to invest buying 2 percent of the company, and she received a substantial salary increase and a promotion.

"But the worst thing was the damage done to individual investors. Hanson created a pyramid scheme that required continual cash infusions. An investor would give him $100,000 in exchange for $1,000 per month interest and a promissory note. Hanson would spend $99,000 on cars, a winery, and other business interests and would then solicit more money so the pyramid building continued. Finally, in May 1988, it all collapsed when enough investors wanted their money back but couldn't get it."

Kroyer's closing argument went on for over a day. It had been a long, fatiguing trial, and at the end he could barely talk. Despite this, he was determined to review the evidence for the jury. He went over every single count and every single document that went with every single exhibit. He knew the case was complicated, and he wanted to make sure the jury convicted Hanson on every count. He later recalled that it was the first time he gave such a detailed closing argument, outlining every piece of evidence that supported the counts charged.

The jury was listening, and they furiously took notes. Kroyer painstakingly cited the elements of burglary, defined as entering a residence with the intent to commit larceny or any felony. Kroyer feared that the jury would think a burglary charge in this case seemed far-fetched and would not convict Hanson of these particular charges. He worried that a lay person's understanding of burglary would be a person entering your home with a mask and gun and robbing you or stealing valuable items from your home. But Kroyer explained that a burglary charge was also justified under the facts of this case. He told them, "Hanson entered an investor's residence intending to sell them investments under false representations. This is entering a residence with intent to steal. This is burglary."

Kroyer knew that if Hanson were convicted of the burglary charges, he would receive a much longer prison term than he would otherwise receive.

Kroyer let the jury know that he would speak to them one more time after Lernhart gave his closing argument. At that time, he would answer any questions raised by the defense, but he assured them there would not be a reasonable doubt as to Hanson's guilt.

Defense attorney Mervin Lernhart, a calm, cerebral man, began his closing arguments by telling the jury that the criminal case against David Hanson was "grossly overcharged, more a product of public wrath over a business failure. Do not convict him because people lost money in a bad business venture." He further argued that Hanson was guilty only of supplying false financial statements to the California real estate commissioner and that the remaining charges were unconnected and unsubstantiated. Hanson's purpose in lying about his company's viability was to obtain a line of credit that would give LendVest ninety days after selling real estate securities to repay the banks or financial institutions that fronted the money.

"Was that right? Probably not," Lernhart admitted. "However, it is not unusual for people seeking bank loans to pad financial statements, and no lenders were at risk."

He then asked the jury to consider that Hanson was experienced in the loan brokerage business and had an impeccable record when he came to Napa and started his company. "His business prospered, and soon he had branch offices because David Hanson and his staff earned the trust of the communities they served."

In 1986, Lernhart explained, the company's income was approximately $500,000, but in an unrelated Internal Revenue Service investigation in 1988, $104,000 was seized from LendVest as part of a drug trafficking and money laundering operation. This money was later returned to LendVest, but the damage was done because word was spread by local media, and that generated a run on the bank in which people called in their notes and other investments. Multimillion-dollar lines of credit from various banks evaporated overnight, resulting in bankruptcy.

Lernhart acknowledged to the jury that the company had a negative worth of $300,000 per year, but this negative net worth was because of expenses connected with a "legitimate and normal business decision to expand the company." He reminded the jury that LendVest was expanding rapidly, from four employees to seventy-five with offices in Rohnert Park and Sacramento.

Further, Lernhart argued, "most people who loaned LendVest money in exchange for unsecured interest-only notes were sophisticated investors who wanted the 13 to 15 percent interest rates Hanson offered. Regardless of what these people say, they knew there was some risk."

The defense attorney then attacked the nature of investors' testimony. "Everyone told the same story, but it is odd that virtually all investor witnesses, including the elderly, had such clear recall about events occurring three or four years ago. When everyone remembers the same conversation, something doesn't feel right." One possible reason, he suggested, was that "people in a relatively small community who lost money through a legitimate business venture had plenty of time for resentment to fester."

Lernhart took on Kroyer's argument that LendVest brokerage was merely a shell game used by Hanson to attract more money. Lernhart said, "Hanson was a longtime Napa resident and a respected businessman. He had seventy-five employees. He had a wife and two children. He had been married nineteen years. Where was he going to go with this scheme? Was he going to get in his Porsche in the middle of the night and drive away? He had a nice lifestyle because of his company's prosperity, not because it was a shell game."

Lernhart finished his closing argument by saying, "Mr. Hanson had a dream, others shared it, and it went a long way toward reality." Lernhart concluded by reminding the jurors that in his opening statement he told them they would have to decide whether this case was about a group of people who lost money on a business venture or whether David Hanson—who spent much of his life in the town—really intended to rip people off. Lernhart submitted that this case was about a group of people who lost money on a business venture and nothing more.

In his rebuttal to the jury, prosecuting attorney Stephen Kroyer was determined to decimate the argument that what Hanson did was largely innocent and that the investors were sophisticated and knew what they were getting into. "Look at what Hanson consciously did. Some victims had money, which Hanson persuaded them to give to him. He took it, paid the interest for several years, and then stopped. These victims lost all their money. Some of these people were living on fixed incomes. They didn't have money in the bank, but they had finally paid off their homes. Hanson convinced them to get a loan against their homes and give that cash to him to buy second deeds of trust from LendVest. These people lost their homes and were forced to go back to work in their seventies. Their retirement was destroyed. In fact, many investors' lives were ruined."

Kroyer concluded by telling the jury that Hanson knew exactly what he was doing. "He was not just ripping people off; he was willing to destroy their lives. He is guilty of the charges brought against him, and you should convict him of those charges."

13

THE VERDICT AND THE SENTENCE

After nine days of deliberation, on October 4, 1991, the jury returned guilty verdicts on sixty-four criminal counts: three burglary counts, fifty-three charges of securities fraud, six counts of embezzlement and theft and two counts of filing false financial statements. Jurors deadlocked on eight other counts, prompting Judge Stephen Mock to declare a mistrial on those counts.

Hanson was immediately handcuffed and taken to jail, and the judge set the date of November 15 for sentencing.

"I'm ecstatic," prosecutor Stephen Kroyer said. "We won as big as we can win." Hanson faced a possible maximum sentence of fifteen years and eight months in state prison.

Defense attorney Mervin Lernhart stated that he would be filing a motion for a new trial because the jury selection process had been interrupted by a Woodland newspaper article about the proceedings.

Eleven of the twelve jurors showed up for the sentencing hearing. This was unusual—jurors who have spent seven weeks in a courtroom listening to evidence usually want to return to their families and their jobs. One juror said, "We've been with this case so long we couldn't miss the sentencing. It's been on our minds."

Many of the victims were also present, and some addressed the judge before he pronounced sentence. Ardis Jabs, an elderly woman, said she was very pleased with the way the trial had gone and hoped Hanson would

Right: Pat Wisknoskie (now Pat Sidorski), a former LendVest loan processor. She lost her entire investment of $27,000. *Courtesy of Pat Sidorski.*

Below: Headline from the October 5, 1991 edition of *The Napa Valley Register* proclaiming Hanson guilty on 64 counts. *Courtesy of the Napa County Library Newspaper Archives.*

receive the maximum sentence. "He took everything from me," she said. "Hanson's sentence will help me end this chapter of my life, and I can hardly wait. It's been devastating."

Pat Wisnoskie, a former LendVest loan processor, said that Hanson was not the nice person he presented to potential investors. "He was an ogre. Everyone was on edge when he walked in." Wisnoskie had lost her entire investment of $27,000, as well as her job.

After everyone who wished to address the judge had completed their comments, a packed courtroom waited for Yolo County Superior Court judge Mock to pronounce sentence.

Speaking directly to Hanson, Judge Mock said, "Your crimes appear to have touched an entire community in a way that crimes of violence seldom do. On one hand, we're only talking about money. But on the other hand,

Headline from the November 15, 1991 edition of the *Napa Valley Register* announcing that Hanson received the maximum sentence. *Courtesy of the Napa County Library Newspaper Archives.*

lives have been fundamentally changed by your behavior. This trial was about that ultimate violation of financial trust."

Hanson showed no expression as the judge delivered his comments.

Just before noon on November 15, 1991, Judge Mock sentenced David Hanson to fifteen years and eight months in state prison. This was the maximum amount of time allowable by law. The judge advised Hanson of his right to appeal his case, and Hanson was then taken by the bailiffs and escorted back to jail to await transport to state prison.

At the conclusion of sentencing, defense attorney Lernhart indicated that his client would appeal the convictions.

Prosecuting attorney Kroyer was satisfied that the prosecution was as successful as it could be and felt that justice was served.

Three years later, on August 22, 1994, in a forty-six-page decision, the Court of Appeal for the Third Appellate District affirmed the judgment of the lower court with one exception: a sentencing error. Punishment on one count was reduced from two years to one year.

Hanson was released from prison after serving his full sentence, less time credited to him for good behavior.

The David Hanson case exposed the greatest financial damage to more victims than any other case in Napa's history. The damage to the victims was not limited to money; damage included the victims' and their families' and friends' emotional suffering, mental anguish, physical debilitation and diminished quality of life. For many of them, Hanson's conduct would remain with them for the rest of their lives.

14

LOOKING BACK

Besides the hundreds of Napa investors who lost vast sums of money from their investments in LendVest, Napa County taxpayers also suffered monetary costs due to the prosecution of this case. At the time the case was brought to court, county officials estimated that it was possible that the cost to the county could be $1 million over the couple of years it would take to defend Robert Pitner and David Hanson. There were 341 criminal charges of securities fraud, theft by embezzlement and burglary—most of them against Hanson.

"It'll have a tremendous effect on the county's budget," said county administrator Jay Hull, explaining that much of the money would have to be taken from the county's contingency fund.

The $1 million estimate was based on the cost of Pitner's and Hanson's court-appointed attorneys, a visiting judge and a change of venue for each defendant. It did not include the district attorney office's prosecution costs.

The reason that Pitner and Hanson were given "free" attorneys to defend themselves was because they had been declared "indigent" by the court, meaning that the court determined that they could not afford to hire private attorneys and must be represented by the county public defender.

Far more than the cost to the county taxpayers, however, was the individual monetary and emotional cost to each of the victims of the fraud perpetrated on them.

The LendVest scandal in the 1980s was devastating to the Napa community. It affected many people both young and old. Many of the victims who were in their seventies and eighties at the time have passed on, but the financial and psychological scars remained with them until their deaths. In many cases, their surviving family members continued to suffer the consequences. Some of the victims who at that time were in their thirties and forties are still alive today, and the vivid memories of the financial crimes that rocked the Napa community and hurt them or their families or friends remain with them.

Thirty-five years after the drug bust on May 24, 1988, which led to the discovery of the crimes perpetuated by David Hanson, some of these surviving victims shared their memories of the scandal.

Tony Ganze, CPA

Today Tony Ganze is a highly regarded certified public accountant (CPA) in Napa. His recollections of the LendVest scandal, when Tony was a young accountant still in his twenties, reveals information that was not known or discovered by the press, nor was it part of the district attorney's formal prosecution—yet it shows how the false financial statements were changed after being accurately prepared by Ganze.

Ganze's statement is as follows:

"Looking back over thirty-five years since the scandal, I have some vivid memories. I started my career right out of college in 1979 in a small CPA firm in Dixon, Illinois. I moved to Napa and on December 1, 1983, I joined John F. Forbes & Company, a regional firm with offices in California, Washington and Oregon. They had acquired Harvey Grant's practice in Napa in July the same year. Harvey was my boss, and he was a person whom I very much looked up to. He was the president of the East Bay chapter of the California CPA Society and highly respected because of his integrity and commitment to excellence.

"Forbes merged with the international firm of Main Hurdman/KMG, the nation's ninth-largest public accounting firm on January 3, 1984. Harvey unmerged his practice shortly thereafter. I chose to stay in Napa instead of moving to San Francisco and continuing with Main Hurdman/KMG.

"LendVest was our largest client. We got business from them and from their employees and investors—they were important to us. I was the one who performed the audit, under Harvey's direction, for LendVest in the early '80s. The audit in 1983, and other years as I recall, confirmed the organization

Tony Ganze and his wife, Teresa, at the Sherry Oven Restaurant prior to its closure. *Courtesy of Tony Ganze.*

was losing money. It also had negative equity. That created a situation where the company could lose its license to broker loans. This required me to issue a going concern report on the audit, thus indicating the entity may not be able to continue. LendVest was required to submit the audit to the Department of Real Estate (DRE). DRE could stop their approval. The reports were completed and submitted to Harvey for signature, who I assumed gave it to David Hanson who would submit to DRE.

"I found out later that Harvey did give my audit to David Hanson, but David objected to the audit report, the loss and negative retained earnings. David somehow persuaded Harvey to prepare false financial statements that would be in compliance with the DRE covenants. I was unaware of the false statements until it came to light in a meeting with the DRE. I was convinced that our firm had performed the audit and issued the report in complete compliance with various regulations and that we would be cleared.

"It wasn't until Harvey called me into his office where we were met by two gentlemen from the DRE of California. They handed me the LendVest financial statements and asked if they were the ones I had prepared. I glanced and said yes. The statement was bound in our firm-embossed cover, had our letterhead and Harvey's signature on the report. I started thumbing through the pages. Whoa! The report did not have the going concern opinion and the statements showed profit and positive retained earnings. I stated that, and the DRE representatives said they had received this report. They said David Hanson had prepared the fraudulent statements. As they talked with Harvey I continued through the statements.

I was in a bit of shock and have no idea what they talked about. After a time, I interrupted. 'Dave Hanson did not prepare these statements. They were prepared by an experienced CPA.' I knew this because only an accountant would know to make all the subtle changes that had to be made to the report and statements so they would not conflict with the other changes that were made. As I explained this to the authorities, it did not occur to me that Harvey might have been that CPA. It was a few days after this meeting that it dawned on me that I never asked Harvey. Of course, when I did, he responded that he had not.

"Sometime after that, Harvey called me into his office. He said he had some bad news. With all that was going on, I was thinking, 'How bad could it be?' He said he just came from his attorney's office and that he needed to confess that he prepared the false statements. I was literally speechless. He then said a couple of things that stuck with me. He said he needed to go home and tell his wife. Then he said, 'I don't know why I did it....No, I don't know why I did it the first time.' I talk to my wife about everything, and I could not imagine that conversation. Harvey's wife and the kids are really wonderful people. And I started to picture how Harvey had gotten himself in a horrible situation by compromising his integrity the first time when the statements were 'just a little out of compliance.' From there it was all downhill. After preparing one false financial statement Harvey was locked in and prepared these financial statements from 1983 to 1988 when the Drug Tug scandal occurred.

"To this day, I like Harvey and wish him the best. He taught me much. He has an incredible family. He had the integrity to come clean and confess everything with complete honesty and a contrite heart. He accepted the price and had the courage to continue on to create another successful business. He never wanted to be a part of this scandal or to hurt anyone but once he prepared one false financial statement he was stuck."

RAYMOND RHODES

Seventy-eight-year-old Raymond Rhodes recalled that he was good friends with the Robinson family. He went to school with Frank Robinson, younger brother of Calvin, and went to the Robinsons' home often in the early '60s. He knew Calvin Robinson as well. He believed the Robinson family were good people.

He remembered that Frank ran the dredging company while Calvin was in prison, but after Calvin got out of prison, he took over the business.

Rhodes had heard many people talking favorably about LendVest as an institution that was paying high interest. Rhodes was attracted to the investment opportunity and ultimately invested $20,000.

When the Drug Tug scandal occurred, Rhodes said, "A light in my brain went on." He thought to himself, "GET YOUR MONEY OUT OF LENDVEST!" But it was too late. When Rhodes went to LendVest and tried to withdraw his money, he was told that LendVest was not a bank, and he couldn't get his money.

Rhodes stated that on looking back at the scandal, what stood out to him was that the man (Charles Duck) who oversaw reorganizing LendVest and helping the investors get their money back was not trustworthy. He also stated that he didn't believe that Hanson initially intended to cheat people, but on reflection he thinks that Hanson, perhaps motivated by greed, got in over his head and found himself in an impossible position. Rhodes feels that the regular employees at LendVest were not influenced by greed and were basically good people who were unaware what was going on.

As to what Hanson would be doing with the drug profits he received, Rhodes speculated that Hanson may have intended to use the profits to pay back the investors to clear up the heavy debt he had created from his Ponzi scheme.

Rhodes also remembered that one of the investors insisted that they use her lawyer to represent them, instead of the RICO lawyer from Denver. He believes this was a mistake.

Rhodes recalled recouping approximately $7,000 of his investment from the bankruptcy court.

Ken Harbison

Harbison, now seventy-seven years old, clearly remembered the case because he refinanced his house to invest $100,000 in LendVest. These funds had been targeted for his young children's future college education. Because he lost his money, he was unable to send his children to the college of their choice.

He recalled that he had to sell his home on Camila Drive, which included a Christmas tree farm on over half an acre of land. At the time, it was worth approximately $400,000; today it would likely be valued at $2 million.

Ken still thinks about that experience and how he got into it in the first place. He said David Hanson was the treasurer of the church to which Ken and his wife, Cindy, belonged. Ken invested because he had confidence in Hanson's financial abilities and because he was attracted to Hanson offering 12 to 14 percent interest on investments with LendVest. Ken also said that he and his wife trusted both David Hanson and Don Lemmons, the chief appraiser at LendVest. To this day, he does not believe that Don Lemmons was as deeply involved. Harbison recalled, "If you knew David Hanson from the church—people spoke highly of him. They said that if you want to make money and you want your money to grow, you would want to talk to David Hanson. He was highly respected for his knowledge of money."

After the local newspaper exposed the seizure of drugs by federal agencies from the tugboat in May 1988 and the connection to LendVest of money laundering allegations, Harbison learned of the Ponzi scheme Hanson was operating at LendVest.

Asked how losing his investment affected his life, Harbison said, "This experience changed my family's lives. We couldn't do as much for our kids as we had hoped. I hated selling our home on Camila Drive because I built it myself." After selling his home, he and his family moved to Lake County, where the cost of living was lower. Today, Ken Harbison is retired and resides with his wife, Cindy, in Tennessee.

Ken Harbison. *Courtesy of Ken Harbison.*

Randy Gourley

Randy Gourley is now in his seventies. His memories centered on his mother, Barbara Gourley, who invested with LendVest. She knew David Hanson personally and invested with him because she trusted him. She mortgaged her house for $110,000 and was told her investment would be secured by a first deed of trust on real estate. In truth and fact, her investment was not secured at all. After news of the scandal broke, Randy's mother found paperwork that showed she had signed a power of attorney to LendVest allowing Hanson to handle the investment. However, Hanson did not secure Barbara's investment.

Randy Gourley. *Courtesy of Randy Gourley.*

The damage to Randy's mother was not limited to her alone. To bail his mom out of her debt and save her home, Randy sold his own real estate investment that was meant to be security for his future. He was planning to build six units on this property, and he was in the middle of the permit process when the scandal broke. So, instead of building this income property for his own financial security, Randy sold the property and paid off his mother's indebtedness on her property so she could keep her home.

In addition to the financial wounds, Randy's mother was angry and depressed. Randy said he is unable to forgive David Hanson, but he has had to let go of his resentment for his own health. When asked if he believed that Hanson intended to cheat his mother, Randy said he believed that then and still does today.

He estimated that there were about four hundred victims, mostly from their church, who applied to get money back from the bankruptcy court. He said, to his recollection, his mother "did not get a penny back from bankruptcy."

ROSA CARPENTER

Judy Taylor, her brother Tom Carpenter and their sister Brenda Phillips remain upset to this day that their late mother, Rosa Carpenter, lost her life savings in the LendVest scandal.

Rosa was a divorced woman when she made the investment with LendVest. She invested her entire life savings, which was over $55,000. She made the investment based on the advice and encouragement of a fellow church member at First Baptist Church. At that time, she was fifty-six years old and worked for the *Napa Valley Register*. Not wanting to be a burden to her children, she continued to work at various jobs until she was eighty-two years old. While she enjoyed working, she found that there was a large difference between wanting to work and needing to work.

Rosa Carpenter. *Courtesy of Judy Taylor.*

Her children were very much aware of the stress that their mother bore in her determination not to be dependent on them.

Rosa's children still have feelings of anger, frustration and sadness when they think about the victimization of their mother by David Hanson.

TOM GORE

Tom Gore worked in the loan department at LendVest from 1983 until May 1988. He specialized in loan origination and was very good at producing and closing loans. He did not invest because he did not have the spare money to do so. He recalled that David Hanson continued to encourage him to invest. Ultimately, Tom agreed to be a 2 percent owner by signing a promissory note, but he never actually put money in, as LendVest went bankrupt soon after.

Tom Gore. *Courtesy of Tom Gore.*

Tom also recalled recommending the investment to his neighbor. Looking back, he is relieved that they said no because he knew that his neighbor would have lost their investment as so many others did.

Tom has a unique recollection of how he learned that something wrong was going on at LendVest. Until that moment, Tom had no clue about any problems with the business or that there were any illegal business practices being conducted. Tom saw a cameraman from a news outlet outside of the Napa LendVest office. Seeing that a film crew was outside the office, Tom went up to Dave Dickson and asked him what was going on. Dickson's face got red, and he closed the blinds of a nearby window. He then looked at Tom and said, "Watch the news tonight."

Unbeknownst to Tom, his uncle had invested $50,000. His uncle later told Tom that he was told his investment was secured by real estate in Vallejo. It turned out that the uncle's investment was not secured. When his uncle later investigated the situation, he learned that David Hanson had initially secured the investment only later to eliminate it.

Tom recalled that David Hanson could be charming and personable, but he was also temperamental. He was serious about doing business and raising money. Tom witnessed David Hanson dressing down employees in front of others in business meetings. Tom stated it was uncomfortable to witness and he believed Hanson's conduct was wrong.

Tom held the belief that David Hanson was "on the up and up, and I wanted to be part of the business." He was unsuspecting and shocked when the truth was revealed.

NAPA MUNICIPAL COURT COMMISSIONER MARC VIEIRA (RET.)

Napa's first Municipal Court commissioner was Marc Vieira, now in his seventies. A commissioner is a judicial officer with less jurisdiction than a judge. Their duties usually were confined to small claims, child support cases, traffic infraction cases and bail hearings. Vieira was appointed to the position after a fine career as a deputy district attorney. He enjoyed substantial success as a Napa prosecutor and was known for his integrity and fairness.

Vieira's only involvement with the LendVest case was at the initial stage of the criminal proceedings. Vieira recalled very little about the case and, to his knowledge, did not personally know any victims or investors. He did recall, however, one vivid memory from when he presided over the arraignment and bail hearing for David Hanson. The arraignment is where the criminal charges are read to the accused by the commissioner. Vieira said in his entire career of presiding over criminal cases, he never had an arraignment with anything close to the number of criminal charges. He could not recall

how many charges there were, but they easily exceeded one hundred. He remembered being so thankful that the lawyers agreed to waive their rights to have him read each criminal count aloud in court.

Vieira stated it was a memorable bail hearing. The courtroom was packed with what Vieira presumed were mostly victims of the fraud. The television networks from San Francisco were in the courtroom filming the hearing. "As the saying goes, you could cut the tension with a knife. It was a lengthy hearing. I don't recall the amount of bail I set, but I do remember that it was the highest bail I ever set for a nonviolent crime."

Marc Vieira. *Courtesy of Marc Vieira.*

Jerry Foster

Seventy-six-year-old Jerry Foster was a police officer who retired in 2003 after thirty years on the Napa Police force.

Jerry recalled that he was assigned to the detective division at the Napa Police Department when Captain Robert Jarecki informed him of the recent DEA Drug Tug bust that had taken place in May 1988. Jerry was assigned to the case involving a mortgage company in Napa called LendVest. His assignment was to assist in the investigation together with district attorney investigator Ed Wynn.

He was ordered to attend a meeting at the Napa County District Attorney's Office that included Napa County district attorney Jerome Mautner, DA investigator Ed Wynn and a State of California investigator assigned by the state to assist with the

Jerry Foster. *Courtesy of Napa Police Historical Society.*

investigation. They were told that previous drug profits from drug smuggling may have been laundered through LendVest. They also learned that many citizens lost their investments with LendVest.

Foster was instructed to interview the citizens who had invested in LendVest and determine what knowledge they had and how they were approached by David Hanson to make these substantial investments. It was at this time that Detective Foster learned that one of the investors was a Napa Police Department sergeant named Joe Masel. Masel's parents had also invested a considerable amount of money. Foster also learned that many of the investors were members of a church congregation to which David Hanson and members of his family belonged.

Foster recalled that during the initial interviews he had with investors, many of them were convinced that their investments were not fraudulent and did not want to believe that they had been duped by Hanson. However, when LendVest closed its doors, Foster noticed how the investors changed their mind.

A common pattern emerged from Foster's interviews with investors. The interviews centered on a scheme. David Hanson would meet a potential investor and present them with a financial prospectus that showed the company to be very sound. When they came to his office, he would place his hand on a large Bible on his desk and swear his commitment to them of a large return on their money. Foster believed that Hanson used his church status and the financial prospectus to lure people to invest their money.

Foster remembered that DA Jerry Mautner was concerned that it would be difficult to prove any fraud against Hanson because initially it did not appear that they could establish David Hanson had any intention of not making good on his deals. They believed he had not been truthful with investors but were uncertain whether they could prove fraud.

However, Foster said the case broke when it became clear through further investigation that the prospectus was not truthful. They found that a CPA, working for Hanson, had set up double financial statements—a false one showing a financially healthy company and a legitimate one showing LendVest was losing substantial sums of money every month. The CPA agreed to cooperate with the police and turned state's evidence against Hanson. Foster said with this turn of events the police were sure that Hanson was defrauding the investors because he knew he did not have the financial assets he represented to the public.

All these years later, Foster remembered that when the officers and investigators had a meeting with DA Jerry Mautner and informed him of their findings, Mautner determined that they could also file multiple counts of burglary against Hanson. Foster said when Mautner said this it sounded strange to Foster, but Foster said that Mautner had a deep understanding of the law and after his explanation he understood that burglary charges were appropriate. This was good news, because it enhanced the possible prison time that Hanson could receive.

This remains, in Jerry Foster's mind, the most serious nonviolent case affecting numerous Napa citizens than any other case he investigated.

DEBRA A. SANDLER

Debra A. Sandler is remarried and is now Debra Daniels. She began working for Napa Valley Mortgage (later LendVest) on Tuolumne Street in Vallejo as a loan processor in late 1986. The company's new building at 1132 Tennessee Street was under construction. When it was finished, Debra recalled that they moved into that building. Debra left the company in the middle of 1988 to work for Central Pacific. She remembered liking her Vallejo boss and fellow employees very much and enjoyed working with them. However, she eventually sought other employment due to negative feelings about the company leadership.

Debra did not invest in LendVest. However, she recalled that an employee presented an offer that the company would loan $25,000 to her to invest in the company. Debra declined the offer. Debra also did not encourage anyone to invest in the company. She remembers to this day the leery feeling she had regarding the owner, David Hanson. She cannot explain why—she calls it intuition. She only saw him three or four times during her employment, at meetings and one holiday dinner. She stated that the other employees at the Vallejo office seemed to worship him. Debra recalled that the other employees in her office were aghast when she refused to contribute to his birthday gift or sign the card.

She believes that he used his position in the church to attract investors.

Debra Sandler, now Debra Daniels. *Courtesy of Debra Daniels.*

No one wanted to believe that a religious person would plan, or do, such despicable acts. He used that to his advantage. She remembers one employee, upon her hiring, invested her entire pension from a previous employer (approximately $250,000). The employee lost her entire investment in LendVest and was devastated.

Today, Debra still remembers the negative feelings she had regarding Hanson but cannot describe what caused those feelings other than intuition. "It was just my internal feelings about the man. There was something about him that made me feel uncomfortable. It was not because of any of his words or actions. I know that seems a little crazy, but I just sense things sometimes."

WAYNE DAVIDSON

Seventy-eight-year-old Wayne Davidson was born and raised in Napa and, except for attending college and serving his country in the Air Force, has lived there his entire life. He became a realtor in 1976, earned his broker's license in 1977 and in 1978, after transforming his family home into office space, opened the doors to Davidson & Bennett Real Estate company. He has served as the secretary, vice president and president of the Board of Realtors.

He recalled the Drug Tug drug scandal and the LendVest Ponzi scheme. He believes David Hanson was intelligent and efficient and very good at

Wayne Davidson. *Photo by the author.*

getting loans for people. He recalled, however, that he was skeptical of the investment part of LendVest. His suspicions were due to the fact that Hanson was paying people 13.5 to 14 percent on their investments when banks were only paying about 5 percent at the time. Wayne did not trust such an interest rate. His reasoning was because of the adage "If it sounds too good to be true, it probably is." Wayne felt that paying such high interest was not possible without some "catch."

MICHAEL R. CRANE

Michael R. Crane, in his seventies and now retired, was a prominent realtor in Napa for many years specializing in agricultural properties. However, as a young man, before going into the real estate profession, he worked for his father at Napa Electric Company. Michael remembers David G. Hanson and believes that he was very good at obtaining loans for his clients. Michael used David G. Hanson to procure a home loan on his new tract home in the Heather Estates subdivision. Michael still remembers that when David Hanson returned Michael's loan application, the income listed was inaccurately high. Michael knew that it was not the amount he had reported, so he informed Hanson that it was not his real income and was too high. Michael also told Hanson that he would not sign the form with the inaccurate income as listed. Hanson agreed to insert the accurate amount and reduced the sum to Michael's true income. Michael said his loan went through successfully even with the lower, accurate income amount listed. However, he never forgot this incident. Looking back, Michael felt that Hanson, or someone at his direction, listed the amount inaccurately high so that the loan would go smoothly and be approved. The incident also showed that Hanson was willing to lie and cheat on a loan application years before the LendVest scandal came to fruition.

Michael R. Crane. *Photo by the author.*

RONALD WALKER

Ron Walker is now seventy-nine years old and is still working at his own construction company, Walker Construction. His dream had been to retire by age forty-five. With that goal in mind, he invested as much as he could in LendVest, a little at a time, from the early '80s until 1988. He trusted David Hanson implicitly. He had built his investment to $340,000 before losing it all when LendVest went bankrupt. The memory of this setback is with him every day.

He holds painful memories about his brother James "Jim" Walker who also invested in LendVest. Jim was very ill at the time the Walker brothers lost their investments. Ron remembered when Jim was on his deathbed, Jim told Ron to "take care of Hanson."

Ron said his brother's deathbed request weighed heavily on him. Once it appeared to Ron that their investments were lost, he felt intense anger toward Hanson. In fact, Ron recalled going over to Hanson's house on Pine Street in Napa with his .45 pistol in his pocket. He was thinking of exacting the ultimate justice for himself, his brother and his community. To his surprise, when Ron arrived at Hanson's house, the front door was open and a party was going on. Ron looked inside the house, and he could see people who appeared to be enjoying themselves. Without knocking, Ron stepped inside the house. As he was contemplating what he was going to do, he heard a voice state clearly, "Don't do it." To this day, he believes God was talking to him. Ron thought better of his actions and left.

Ron recalled many people attempted to console him about his financial loss, telling him, "You can write it off." Ron said he checked it out with his accountant but was unable to "write it off."

Ron did not get any of his investment back from the bankruptcy court. However, he was part of a lawsuit that pursued financial remedies against an accounting firm connected to LendVest. As a result of this lawsuit, Ron recovered 33 percent of his investment. He felt fortunate that he didn't lose everything.

With the passage of time, Ron is no longer angry or depressed. In fact, Ron believes that the fact that he kept working probably benefited him in the long run. It keeps him going, and he believes that has contributed to his still being alive. After he believed he heard God's voice, his faith deepened. He considers himself a devout Christian to this day.

Ron was encouraged by other people's humanity. He recalled that when he lost his investment, he was unable to pay his own mortgage. One of Ron's customers, who learned of Ron's setback, paid him early, before Ron had completed the job, and this enabled Ron to meet his bills. He never forgot the kindness of this friend.

Ron believed then, and still does to this day, that Hanson was a shrewd businessman and took care of him over the years. He thinks that Hanson got in over his head and speculates that Hanson intended to take the drug profits and pay all his investors in full. However, that never happened. Greed got in the way of his plan.

Ron acknowledged that Hanson cheated people, and his conduct hurt hundreds of families. He recalled from the meetings he attended that there were 325 families who lost their life savings or homes due to the actions and greed of Hanson.

Ron stated that he forgave David Hanson, but he cannot forgive the sin that hurt so many people. Ron believes Hanson should have contacted him when he was released from prison to apologize to him and ask for his forgiveness. But to this day, that has never happened.

JANE LEMMONS

Jane Lemmons was the wife of Roy Lemmons, who was a first cousin of Don Lemmons, the former vice president and chief appraiser at LendVest. She knew Don Lemmons and was aware of the LendVest scandal not only from an insider's perspective as a relative by marriage but also as an investor.

To this day, her memories remain etched clearly in her mind. She still experiences feelings of bitterness. She told her husband she did not want to invest in LendVest, but her husband pressured her. She stated that her father had recently paid off Jane and Roy's house, and Jane did not want to again put a mortgage on their home that was now owned free and clear. Jane said she was concerned that David Hanson was not on the "up and up," but her husband countered, "Well, my cousin Don Lemmons works there, and he would not cheat us." Consequently, after much pressure from her husband, Roy, they refinanced their home to obtain $100,000, which they then invested in LendVest. Of course, they lost their full investment.

Jane was angry after the loss of their investment, but she refused to lose their home. She continued to work for years to pay off the debt, and she eventually did pay the indebtedness in full after her husband, Roy, died. She remains proud that she paid the debt and did not allow this financial setback to take her home away from her.

Jane has had a difficult time letting go of her anger, although she knows she should for her own mental health. She divulged that one time when she saw David Hanson at Zeller's hardware store in Napa, she found herself picking up an axe from a shelf in the store. Her intention was to hit him over the head, but she backed off quickly when she thought better of it.

Jane continues to fight her bitterness. She believes her faith in God has helped her as she continues to work on forgiveness, and she acknowledges that even though the memories are still with her she is coping much better now than in the past.

JAMES V. JONES

James V. Jones was a prominent attorney in Napa who practiced law from 1967 to 2020. He was a U.S. Navy veteran: amphibious force, gunnery officer and a member of the Naval Security Group. He was a Napa City Council member from 1972 to 1976 and president of the Napa County Bar Association in 1977. He cofounded the law firm Jones, Gaw and Van Male in 1972. He was the Boy Scout district chairman in 1972 and 2003–10; an elder at the First Presbyterian Church; and the past lieutenant governor of Kiwanis. He is currently serving on the Salvation Army and Community Action Napa Valley Boards and the Golden Gate Council BSA (Boy Scouts of America) advisory board. He is also currently a trustee of the Napa County law library.

James V. Jones. *Photo by the author.*

As a lawyer, Jones appeared before the California Supreme Court in *People v. Roads (1968) 275 CA2nd 593*. It was a first-degree murder case in which for the first time in California a murder indictment was overturned. Jones was also involved in the case of *People v. Mentzer (1985) 163 CA 3rd 482*, in which the court redefined the law of arson for the first time since 1873.

Jones was a practicing Napa lawyer during the entire time that LendVest existed. He recalled, "I represented several clients who were severely injured in the LendVest mess. Some invested money they got by mortgaging their houses. Another man pulled all his retirement funds out of STRS (State Teachers Retirement System) and invested it into LendVest. As far as I know they all lost all of their money."

Jones continued, "The scheme was simple enough. Investors thought that they were investing in a 'can't lose' proposition. Their money would be invested into residential real property. They would be in first position on the title of a home or homes whose value was backed up by recent appraisals, which they would be shown. Their monthly payments would be at 12 percent, at a time when similar loans were going at 14 percent. This made it seem that the loan program in which they were involved was not 'predatory' nor overly aggressive. At the time, a loan in first position on properly valued California residential real property was probably as good as gold. All of this was run through First American Title Company, a respected national business. How could it go wrong?"

Jones reviewed the voluminous stack of loan documents that his clients provided him. In the mounds of documents he read, Jones observed that all his clients had signed a power of attorney. The clients told Jones that when occasionally someone asked what the power of attorney was for, they were told that it was part of the LendVest total customer care operation. They were told that the power of attorney would simplify transactions so that the investment would go smoothly and save the client from coming back to LendVest to sign other paperwork. LendVest would do this for them as an additional service to the client. What Jones's clients were not told was that the power of attorney would be used to undo the client's security.

As the depth of this scheme became clear to Jones, he urged the district attorney to act. The DA told Jones that he wanted a smoking gun. Jones then sent his clients who had been defrauded to the DA for his review. Eventually, enough solid evidence of this complex web of fraud was obtained. Charges were filed, and convictions were obtained.

AFTERWORD

My intent when I began to write the story of LendVest was to set forth in detail the Ponzi scheme that affected a multitude of Napa citizens and the residual financial devastation to these people and their families. Part I of this book ("The Drug Tug") was written for the sole purpose of explaining to the reader how the seizure of the drugs from the barge and the resultant money laundering (technically called currency structuring) was connected to Napa and, specifically, to LendVest.

However, throughout the writing of this story, I often wondered who was behind the drug smuggling. Was it only Calvin Robinson's scheme, aided by his young crew? Or were there others involved? Was there a larger criminal organization backing the plot?

Certainly, the federal trials regarding the smuggling gave no clarity. This is likely because the federal prosecutors were focused on the people charged with drug smuggling—that is, Calvin Robinson and his crew. The *reason* for the drug smuggling was not at issue and did not have to be proved. And the defense certainly presented no evidence on the background of the smuggling operation—it merely denied knowledge of the existence of the contraband on the barge. I was left, however, with the nagging question of how this smuggling plot was planned, financed and executed and by whom. Was David Hanson or any other LendVest employee connected to the drug smuggling, other than their part in the currency structuring? Did they use investors' money to fund the operation? How deep did this go with LendVest?

The answer to my query came from my interview with Dr. Norman Wood, a former federal agent who had investigated the drug smuggling case. What he told me was astounding but uncorroborated. However, in interviewing him about his background—and knowing he was a chief witness in the federal drug smuggling trials—I came to believe that he was a reliable source. In addition to my interviews with Dr. Wood, he provided many photographs from the investigation. Norman Wood was a West Virginia state trooper when he was recruited to attend the Federal Law Enforcement Training Center in Georgia. From there, he was hired by the U.S. Customs Service as an investigator for the drug smuggling plot. His candid, forthright interviews

Dr. Norman Wood.
Courtesy of Norman Wood.

with me were critical to understanding why there were two Drug Tug smuggling operations: a successful one on the *Ruby R* tugboat in 1987 and the unsuccessful operation on the *Intrepid Venture* that resulted in the May 1988 drug bust in San Francisco Bay.

Concisely stated, the purpose of the drug smuggling operations was to raise money for a Russian plot supported by the KGB to overthrow Russian leader Mikhail Gorbachev. To accomplish this goal, large sums of money had to be raised—hence the selling of drugs. Yes, the Drug Tug smuggling was, in fact, a Russian operation. How much knowledge of this plot was known to LendVest's employees is unclear. Wood believes that Calvin Robinson did not tell his sisters Sue and Donna or his brother-in-law Don Lemmons about the Russian involvement. Without Don Lemmons's knowledge of the Russian involvement, no one else at LendVest could have known about it.

Starting his investigation with very little information, Norman Wood managed to discover the work being done by Calvin Robinson and his crew members in the delta to ready the tugs and barges for the trips to obtain the drugs from a mother ship near Hawaii, which, in turn, would raise money to fund the attempted coup. Agent Wood conducted surveillance on Calvin Robinson and his crew members for about a year.

Below is the statement Norman Wood provided to me in 2023:

> *This was the most complex case I had ever been involved with. The players involved went from local individuals from Napa to the Russian*

military who controlled Afghanistan, and all the way to the KGB in the Kremlin. The goal of this operation was to remove Mikhail Gorbachev from power in 1989. To do that they needed money, $100 million. To get the money, they were going to smuggle one hundred tons of Afghan hashish into San Francisco. Using a former U.S. intelligence operative, Thomas Gary Smith, and a career criminal, Calvin Robinson, who helped convicted Russian spy Christopher Boyce escape from Lompoc prison, they devised an ingenious plan that was foolproof. Almost. Timing was critical, and we were somehow able to complete this mission successfully when all the odds were stacked against us. From what we were able to do, the coup was postponed until 1991, at which time it failed. I left the government in 1992 to return to West Virginia to attend medical school.

Wood also revealed the identities of the key Russian players. They were General Valin Varennikov, Marshal Dmitry Yazov and Head of Foreign Intelligence Vladimir Kryuchkov. They called their inner circle Red Sword. Varennikov oversaw getting the hashish out of Afghanistan. President Ronald Reagan wanted to protect Gorbachev and his march toward democracy. Gorbachev and his liberal policies were good for the United States but not good for the oligarchy in the USSR. Gorbachev brought about the fall of the USSR and an end to the Cold War after the failed coup in 1991. All the conspirators were arrested and took a plea deal except for General Varennikov. He refused and wanted to go to trial. He was finally acquitted by their Supreme Court.

Calvin was brought into this Russian plot through his connection to Christopher Boyce, a spy for Russia. Boyce is the person who introduced Calvin to the KGB. Christopher Boyce and Calvin Robinson were cellmates at the federal prison in Lompoc, California. Calvin was paroled a couple of months before Christopher Boyce climbed the fence and escaped. It was Calvin who took Christopher to Bonners Ferry, Idaho, and hid him out with his old girlfriend Gloria White. Calvin and Billy Lytle (Calvin's cousin and former bank robber) taught Christopher and Gloria how to rob banks at her cabin on Katka Mountain. Christopher and Gloria hit several banks in the Pacific Northwest to get money. Calvin and Billy Lytle were to find a vessel to purchase with the money and then smuggle Christopher out of the United States and to a Russian vessel. Boyce wanted to be an officer in the KGB if he could get there. And they almost did it. But Christopher got sloppy and was running his mouth in a local bar in Bonners Ferry, and a fellow called the U.S. Marshals. Boyce was apprehended and returned to prison.

Thomas Gary Smith was a former CIA officer who went to Cali, Colombia, with Calvin Robinson in 1986 to introduce him to KGB's Head of Foreign Intelligence Vladimir Kryuchkov and set up the logistics for the two smuggling operations. Thomas Gary Smith had been stationed in Afghanistan, where he had been involved in smuggling drugs with Kryuchkov. Kryuchkov had been Christopher Boyce's contact in Russia. Smith is the one who contacted Boyce's former attorney, who, in turn, is the person who set up Dredge Masters Inc. and contacted Calvin in the beginning.

It is unknown whether Calvin knew of the planned coup. What is clear, however, is that Calvin's role was that of a drug mule, responsible for transportation of the drugs, for which he expected to be paid $2 million. The first drug smuggling occurred around August or September 1987, and the second was in May 1988.

It seems that Norman Wood knew Calvin quite well but from a distance. Wood spoke to Robinson twice while undercover, having followed him almost daily for over a year. Interestingly, from a distance, Wood said that Robinson seemed polite and personable. His crew seemed to like him, and he had several girlfriends. He was not a violent man and never carried a gun, although there was a shotgun on the *Intrepid Venture*. Wood also stated that Calvin was a professional career criminal. Robinson knew what he was doing, and he was very smart about it. He had a heightened sense of paranoia, always watching to see if law enforcement was on to him. Wood didn't have any correspondence with Calvin until after 2019, when Wood helped to obtain a compassionate release from prison for Calvin.

Dr. Wood stated, "In 2019, I was contacted by Cait Boyce, former wife of Christopher Boyce. I was advised that Calvin Robinson was dying of cancer in federal prison. The Parole Board had recommended a Compassionate Release, but the Federal Justice had so far declined to sign it. After reviewing Mr. Robinson's medical records, I wrote a letter to Senior Federal Justice Charles Breyer, Northern District, California. After receiving my letter, Justice Breyer signed Calvin Robinson's Compassionate Release.

Calvin and I communicated several times after his release. On September 24, 2023, Calvin's wife, Tina, informed me that Calvin passed away at his home in Oregon on September 23, 2023."

For readers interested in more information about the Russian plot, Norman Wood has written a four-book fiction series, The Red Sword Series, based on the 1988 drug smuggling operation that resulted in the foiling of the Russian attempted coup. Wood stated that names have been changed, but the account, while fictional, closely follows the actual events of the Russian operation.

BIBLIOGRAPHY

Books

Wood, Norman. *Red Sword.* Bellingham, WA: Bookhouse Publishing, 2021.
————. *Thorn.* Bellingham, WA: Bookhouse Publishing, 2022.

Newspapers and Periodicals

Mac Lennan, Ken. "Follow the Money: The Drug Tug Bust and the LendVest Scandal." *Napa County Historical Society: Gleanings* 6, no. 1 (April 2008).
Napa Valley Register. "Napa-Tied 30-Ton Hash Bust." May 24, 1988.
————. "Drug Probe Deep into Napa." May 25, 1988.
————. "Suspect's Sister Charged." May 26, 1988.
————. "2 Napans Held in Drug Case." May 26, 1988.
————. "Laundering Scandal Spreads." May 27, 1988.
————. "2nd Tug Seized in Hashish Case." May 27, 1988.
————. "Pitner Was Duped, Attorney Says." May 28, 1988.
————. "Robinson's Attorney Raps Federal Acts." May 28, 1988.
————. "Lawyer Blames Hanson." May 30, 1988.
————. "State Auditors Checking LendVest." May 31, 1988.
————. "Nervousness at LendVest." June 1, 1988
————. "Shake Up at Top of LendVest." June 1, 1988.

————. "Staff Laid Off by LendVest." June 2, 1988.

————. "Agents Probing Land Transactions." June 3, 1988.

————. "Drug Tug IRS Seizes Napa Fund." June 4, 1988.

————. "Lend Vest Being Sued for Savings." June 6, 1988.

————. "Find of Cash Tied to Drugs." June 7, 1988.

————. "Lend Vest Plans Meeting." June 7, 1988.

————. "Drug Case Indictment Obtained." June 8, 1988.

————. "Meeting Tonight on LendVest Plan." June 9, 1988.

————. "Robinsons Enter Pleas of Innocent." June 9, 1988.

————. "Sue Lemmons Posts $500,000 Bail." June 11, 1988.

————. "Investors Hit at LendVest." June 14, 1988.

————. "Federal Indictment Based on Chronology of Events." June 15, 1988.

————. "Money Structuring: Surrender After Indictments." June 15, 1988.

————. "Not Guilty Pleas in LendVest Case." June 16, 1988.

————. "LendVest Investors Say Liquidate, Don't Reorganize." June 17, 1988.

————. "Friday Hearing Scheduled in LendVest Bankruptcy." June 21, 1988.

————. "LendVest Granted Short Lease on Life." June 24, 1988.

————. "LendVest Trustee Will Know More in 30 Days." June 25, 1988.

————. "Robinson Tied to Colombia." June 29, 1988.

————. "Not Guilty Pleading by Dredge Masters." June 30, 1988.

————. "Robinson Loses Plea for Bail." July 2, 1988.

————. "Blame Put on Hanson." July 7, 1988.

————. "New Attitude from LendVest." July 7, 1988.

————. "Bankruptcy at Mathews Complex." July 21, 1988.

————. "Lemmons' Lawyers Not in Conflict, Judge Rules." July 21, 1988.

————. "Ex-Workers Suing LendVest." August 4, 1988.

————. "LendVest Gets Chance to Save Itself." August 10, 1988.

————. "Suits Claim Drug Links in LendVest." August 16, 1988.

————. "Creditors Will Meet on LendVest Future." August 20, 1988.

————. "Fraud Probe in LendVest." August 22, 1988.

————. "Funds Short in LendVest." August 23, 1988.

————. "Attorney Makes Bid for LendVest Lawsuit." August 24, 1988.

————. "LendVest Shut Down." September 1, 1988.

————. "Dickson Says He Will Testify for Prosecution." October 12, 1988.

———. "Ex-LendVest Head Files for Bankruptcy." November 3, 1988.

———. "Feds Admit 'Drug Tug''Investigator Misconduct." November 8, 1988.

———. "Creditors Could Force LendVest into Liquidation." December 14, 1988.

———. "Napa DA with Probe of LendVest." December 21, 1988.

———. "LendVest Story Carries into 1989." January 2, 1989.

———. "Mathews Winery Giving Up." January 10, 1989.

———. "Drug Trial Begins Monday." January 21, 1989.

———. "LendVest Creditors Must Refile." January 21, 1989.

———. "Robinson Relatives on Trial." January 23, 1989.

———. "2 Napans Listed as 'Drug Tug' Possible Jurors." January 24, 1989.

———. "Robinson to Be Tried Separately." January 26, 1989.

———. "Duck Quits but No Effect on LendVest." February 6, 1989.

———. "Robinson Opens His Own Defense." February 7,1989.

———. "'Drug Tug' Haul $1 Billion-Agent." February 9, 1989.

———. "'Drug Tug' Agent to Return to Stand." February 10, 1989.

———. "Fibers Implicate Tug Crew." February 11, 1989.

———. "Case Opened by Robinson." February 16, 1989.

———. "Robinson Figures to Take Stand Soon." February 21, 1989.

———. "Robinson Rests, Fate Up to Jury." February 22, 1989.

———. "Robinson Found Guilty, Others May Alter Pleas." February 23, 1989.

———. "'Drug Tug' Trial Delay, It's Put Off Week." February 27, 1989.

———. "No Liquidation for LendVest Yet." March 7, 1989.

———. "Officer Credited with Helping Break 'Drug Tug' Takes Stand." March 25, 1989.

———. "Robinson to Blame." April 1, 1989.

———. "Possible Hung Jury in 'Drug Tug.'" April 11, 1989.

———. "Jury Acquits Crew of 'Drug Tug.' April 12, 1989.

———. "LendVest Jury Selection Starts Today." April 17, 1989.

———. "LendVest Jury Selection Continues." April 18, 1989.

———. "LendVest Trustee Duck Told to Deliver Records." April 18, 1989.

———. "Jury Ready to Hear LendVest Trial." April 19, 1989.

———. "LendVest Trial Starts; Lawyers Address Jury." April 24, 1989.

———. "LendVest Trial: A Case of Trust?" April 25, 1989.

———. "LendVest Money Vanished." April 26, 1989.

————. "Attorneys Fail to Win Mistrial." April 27, 1989.

————. "Witness Describes LendVest Fall." April 29, 1989.

————. "Hanson Stories Differed." May 2, 1989.

————. "Crucial Testimony in LendVest." May 5, 1989.

————. "IRS Agent Testifies About Hanson." May 9, 1989.

————. "LendVest Trial Focus on Money." May 10, 1989.

————. "LendVest Trustee Duck Ordered to Free Papers." May 10, 1989.

————. "Lend Vest Defense Blames Calvin." May 11, 1989.

————. "LendVest Defense Sets Foundation." May 13, 1989.

————. "LendVest Trustee Takes the Fifth." May 16, 1989.

————. "Lend Vest Defense: 'I Was Threatened.'" May 16, 1989.

————. "LendVest Trustee Duck Steps Down." May 19, 1989.

————. "Hanson Proclaims Innocence." May 23, 1989.

————. "Big SF Trial in Last Stages." May 24, 1989.

————. "Drug Tug Case Broke 1 Year Ago." May 24, 1989.

————. "LendVest Trial in Its Last Stages." June 1, 1989.

————. "LendVest Testimony Ends Dramatically." June 3, 1989.

————. "Federal Judge Hands Robinson Maximum Term." June 9, 1989.

————. "LendVest Jury Taking Its Time." June 13, 1989.

————. "LendVest Jury Finds Hanson, Pitner Guilty." June 15, 1989.

————. "Mathews Winery Offer Made." June 15, 1989.

————. "School Victim of Scandal." June 15, 1989.

————. "LendVest Fraud Investigations Taking Shape." June 17, 1989.

————. "Proposed Mathews Buyer Short of Funding." July 27, 1989.

————. "Sentencing Due in LendVest Case." August 8, 1989.

————. "Sue Lemmons to Trial Again." August 11, 1989.

————. "LendVest Sentencing Scheduled." September 14, 1989.

————. "Sentencing in Hanson and Pitner Delayed." September 15, 1989.

————. "LendVest Trustee Duck Arraigned." September 25, 1989.

————. "Duck Plans Guilty Plea." September 26, 1989.

————. "Big Auction at Mathews Could Cost." September 28, 1989.

————. "Charles Duck Sued in Marin County Case." September 29, 1989.

————. "Hanson, Pitner Facing Charges." December 24, 1989.

————. "Hanson Locked Up While Pitner Sought." December 25, 1989.

———. "Court Appearances for Hanson, Pitner." December 26, 1989.

———. "Hanson and Pitner Stay Behind Bars." December 27, 1989.

———. "Alleged Victims Voice Bitterness." December 27, 1989.

———. "Hanson, Pitner Denied Their Freedom." December 28, 1989.

———. "LendVest Case Will Cost Taxpayers." January 15, 1990.

———. "Bankruptcy Judge Waits on LendVest Decisions." January 22, 1990.

———. "Lend Vest Funds Sought of State." January 31, 1990.

———. "Lemmons Pleads Guilty in S.F. Court." March 19, 1990.

———. "Another Legal Action in LendVest Case." April 5, 1990.

———. "Judge Says 'Denied' to Hanson Bail Request." May 26, 1990.

———. "It's Perez as DA and 'No' to Measure A." June 6, 1990.

———. "Hanson, Pitner Face Sentencing Today." June 7, 1990.

———. "Tearful Pitner Given 'Benefit of the Doubt.'" June 8, 1990.

———. "Judge Calls LendVest Scandal 'Tragedy.'" June 14, 1990.

———. "Hanson Wants New Attorneys." June 18, 1990.

———. "Gag Order Issued by Judge in LendVest Case." June 19, 1990.

———. "Sue Lemmons Given Probation." June 22, 1990.

———. "LendVest Witnesses Point to Hanson." June 23, 1990.

———. "LendVest Preliminary Hearing: A Day-by-Day Look at Week One." June 23, 1990.

———. "LendVest: Week II." July 7, 1990.

———. "Witnesses at LendVest Hearing Speak of Trust, Money and Hanson." July 7, 1990.

———. "Perez Makes Plans Prior to Taking Office." July 8, 1990.

———. "Robert Pitner the Focus of Third Week of LendVest Hearing." July 21, 1990.

———. "Witnesses Tell of Huge LendVest Losses." July 21, 1990.

———. "Former LendVest Accountant Takes Stand, Stays Quiet." August 6, 1990.

———. "'Drug Tug' Skipper Says Government at Fault." August 30, 1990.

———. "Court Upholds Calvin Robinson's Conviction." September 1, 1990.

———. "LendVest Hearing Resumes Wednesday After Month Delay." September 4, 1990.

———. "Hanson and Pitner Face Trial." September 6, 1990.

———. "Perez Takes Over DA's Office." January 7, 1991.

———. "LendVest Charges on Pitner Dismissed." February 22, 1991.

———. "No Contest Plea Offered by LendVest Accountant." March 21, 1991.

———. "LendVest Victims Get Some Money." April 25, 1991.

———. "Doubt Voiced on LendVest Settlement." May 8, 1991.

———. "Investors' Lawsuit Against LendVest Heads into Trial." June 24, 1991.

———. "Hanson LendVest Trial Starts Monday." July 28, 1991.

———. "Hanson Trial Delay Caused by Article." August 2, 1991.

———. "Attorney Says Media Helped Cause Failure of LendVest." August 6, 1991.

———. "Lawyers Paint Vastly Different Pictures of David Hanson." August 6, 1991.

———. "CPA Traces Trail of Money Trouble." August 7, 1991.

———. "Employee: Hanson Said Alter the Books." August 7, 1991.

———. "LendVest Investors Testify at Woodland Trial." August 8, 1991.

———. "Accountant: Hanson Drew Huge Salary." August 8, 1991.

———. "Testimony Reveals Not Every LendVest Victim Was Elderly." August 9, 1991.

———. "Hanson Hit by Damaging Testimony." August 13, 1991.

———. "Lend Vest Investors Continue Testimony in Woodland Trial." August 13, 1991.

———. "LendVest Employee Who Invested Testifies." August 14, 1991.

———. "They'll Get 25 Cents on the Dollar if They Vote Yes." August 15, 1991.

———. "Ex-Airport Director Testifies Against Hanson." August 16, 1991.

———. "Personal Costs High in Case." August 17, 1991.

———. "Testimony Covers Link Between LendVest and Winery." August 20, 1991.

———. "Employee Who Didn't Buy Stock Became Pariah." August 20, 1991.

———. "Religion Swayed Some Investors." August 21, 1991.

———. "Hanson 'Burglar,' Prosecutor Says." August 21, 1991.

———. "61 Counts Dismissed." August 22, 1991.

———. "Hanson Had Help with Deals, Witnesses Testify." August 22, 1991.

———. "Former Hanson Attorney Plans to Testify at Trial." August 23, 1991.

———. "Judge Denies Motion to Dismiss Trial." September 10, 1991.

————. "Pitner's Trial Delayed." September 10, 1991.

————. "Hanson Defense Opens in LendVest Trial." September 11, 1991.

————. "Defense Witnesses Claim Panic Destroyed Company." September 13, 1991.

————. "Witness Says LendVest Was Stable." September 13, 1991.

————. "Hanson Will Not Take the Stand." September 17, 1991.

————. "Mrs. Hanson Takes Stand to Defend Husband." September 17, 1991.

————. "Witness: IRS Prevented LendVest from Making Payroll." September 17, 1991.

————. "Lawyers Give Closing Arguments in Hanson Fraud Trial." September 20, 1991.

————. "Lend Vest Defense Arguments Monday." September 21, 1991.

————. "Hanson Defense Closes." September 24, 1991.

————. "Hanson Waits for Word from Jurors." October 1, 1991.

————. "Juror Gets a Break from Judge." October 1, 1991.

————. "Hanson: Guilty on 64 Counts." October 4, 1991.

————. "What's Happened to Other Former LendVest Officials?" October 6, 1991.

————. "Hanson Gets the Maximum." November 15, 1991.

Unpublished Works

Criminal Case Number 12526 (Yolo County). People vs. David Hanson. Napa County District Attorney's documents.

Crane, Michael. Oral interviews with author. Napa, CA. June 2023.

Davidson, Wayne. Oral interviews with author. Napa, CA. June 2023.

Decision. Court of Appeal of California, Third Appellate District. Decision dated August 22, 1994.

Fallon, Michael. Oral interviews with author. Napa, CA. May 27, 28 and 30, 2023, and June 15, 2023.

Foster, Jerry. Oral interview with author. Napa, CA. March 3, 2023.

Gore, Tom. Oral interview with author. Napa, CA. February 28, 2023.

Gourley, Randy. Oral interview with author. Napa, CA. February 28, 2023.

Harbison, Ken. Email interviews with author. Napa, CA. January 18, 2022; April 25, 2022; and May 5, 2022.

Jones, James V. Oral interviews with author. Napa, CA. February 28, 2023, and March 1, 2023.

Kroyer, Judge Stephen T. (Ret.). Oral interview with author. Napa, CA. July 9, 2020.

Lemmons, Jane. Telephone interview with author. Napa, CA. July 20, 2022.

Lernhart, Mervin. Oral interview with author. Napa, CA. July 24, 2020.

Olsen, Steven M. Telephone interviews with author. Napa, CA. June 8 and 13, 2023.

Rhodes, Raymond. Oral interviews with author. Napa, CA. March 5, 12 and 14, 2023.

Sandler Daniels, Debra. Oral interview with author. Napa, CA. March 20 and 22, 2023.

Sidorski, John. Oral interview with author. Napa, CA October 10, 2020.

Taylor, Judy. Oral interview with author. Napa, CA. June 12, 2023.

Vieira, Marc. Oral interview with author. Napa, CA. August 16, 2023.

Walker, Ron. Oral interview with author. Napa, CA. February 27, 2023.

Wisnoskie Sidorski, Pat. Oral interview with author. Napa, CA. October 6, 2020.

Wood, Norman. Email interviews with author. August 2023.

Wynn, Ed. Oral interview with author. Napa, CA. July 20, 2020, and September 8, 2020.

ABOUT THE AUTHOR

Photo by Ann Guadagni.

Raymond A. Guadagni was raised in Napa, California. He graduated from the University of California at Berkeley in 1968 and from Hastings College of Law (now UC College of the Law, San Francisco) in 1971. He practiced as a deputy public defender in Stockton, California, for three years before returning to his hometown in 1975 to establish a law practice. On November 1, 1995, Guadagni became Napa's first Superior Court commissioner, and in 2001 he was appointed Superior Court judge for the County of Napa. He retired in 2012 and now serves as an assigned judge with the Temporary Assigned Judges Program of California.

He is married with two adult daughters and five grandchildren. He enjoys writing, music, travel and spending time with his family.